Level 3 • Book 1

Friendship

•

City Wildlife

•

Imagination

SRA OPEN COURT READING

Level 3 • Book 1

— PROGRAM AUTHORS —

Marilyn Jager Adams   Iva Carruthers   Marsha Roit

Carl Bereiter   Jan Hirshberg   Marlene Scardamalia

Joe Campione   Anne McKeough   Gerald H. Treadway, Jr.

Marcy Stein   Michael Pressley

A Division of The McGraw·Hill Companies

Columbus, Ohio

Acknowledgments

Grateful acknowledgment is given to the following publishers and copyright owners for permissions granted to reprint selections from their publications. All possible care has been taken to trace ownership and secure permission for each selection included. In case of any errors or omissions, the Publisher will be pleased to make suitable acknowledgments in future editions.

From STORIES JULIAN TELLS by Ann Cameron and illustrated by Ann Strugnell, copyright © 1981 by Ann Cameron. Illustrations copyright © 1981 by Ann Strugnell. Used by permission of Alfred A. Knopf, an imprint of Random House Children's Books, a division of Random House, Inc.

From Angel Child, Dragon Child, by Michele Maria Surat. © 1983 by Raintree/Steck-Vaughn. All rights reserved. Reproduced by arrangement with Steck-Vaughn Company.

JANEY by Charlotte Zolotow. COPYRIGHT © 1973 BY CHARLOTTE ZOLOTOW. Used by permission of HarperCollins Publishers.

"The Tree House" from THE BIG BOOK OF PEACE. Reprinted by permission of Harold Ober Associates Incorporated. Copyright © 1990 by Lois Lowry. Illustration © Trina Schart Hyman.

RUGBY & ROSIE by Nan Rossiter. Copyright © Nan Rossiter, 1997. Published by arrangement with Dutton Children's Books, a member of Penguin Group (USA) Inc.

TEAMMATES by Peter Golenbock, text copyright © 1990 by Golenbock Communications, illustrations copyright © 1990 by Paul Bacon, used with permission of Harcourt, Inc.

"The Legend of Damon and Pythias" from THE BAG OF FIRE AND OTHER PLAYS by Fan Kissen. Copyright © 1964 by Houghton Mifflin Company, renewed © 1993 by John Kissen Heaslip. Reprinted by permission of Houghton Mifflin Company. All rights reserved.

From THE BOY WHO DIDN'T BELIEVE IN SPRING by Lucille Clifton, copyright © 1973 by Lucille Clifton, text. Used by permission of Dutton's Children's Books, an imprint of Penguin Putnam Books for Young Readers, a division of Penguin Putnam Inc.

"City Critters: Wild Animals Live in Cities, Too" from 3-2-1 CONTACT Magazine, Sept. 1988. Copyright 1988 Sesame Workshop (New York, New York). All rights reserved.

"Raccoon" from THE LLAMA WHO HAD NO PAJAMA: 100 FAVORITE POEMS, copyright © 1973 by Mary Ann Hoberman, reprinted by permission of Harcourt, Inc.

From MAKE WAY FOR DUCKLINGS by Robert McCloskey, copyright 1941, renewed © 1969 by Robert McCloskey. Used by permission of Viking Penguin, an imprint of Penguin Putnam Books for Young Readers, a division of Penguin Putnam Inc.

From URBAN ROOSTS by Barbara Bash. Copyright © 1990 by Barbara Bash. By permission of Little, Brown and Company.

"The Worm" by Raymond Souster is reprinted from COLLECTED POEMS OF RAYMOND SOUSTER by permission of Oberon Press.

"Pigeons" from I THOUGHT I HEARD THE CITY by Lilian Moore. Copyright © 1969 Lilian Moore. © renewed 1997 Lilian Moore Reavin. Reprinted by permission of Marian Reiner for the author.

TWO DAYS IN MAY by Harriet Peck Taylor, pictures by Leyla Torres. Copyright © 1999 by Harriet Peck Taylor, illustrations copyright © 1999 by Leyla Torres. Reprinted by permission of Farrar, Straus & Giroux, LLC.

SECRET PLACE by Eve Bunting, illustrated by Ted Rand. Text copyright © 1996 by Eve Bunting. Illustrations copyright © 1996 by Ted Rand. Reprinted by permission of Clarion Books/Houghton Mifflin Co. All rights reserved.

THROUGH GRANDPA'S EYES TEXT COPYRIGHT © 1980 BY PATRICIA MACLACHLAN. ILLUSTRATIONS COPYRIGHT © 1980 BY DEBORAH KOGAN RAY. Used by permission of HarperCollins Publishers.

Text of "The Apple" from EATS by Arnold Adoff. COPYRIGHT © 1979 BY ARNOLD ADOFF. Used by permission of HarperCollins Publishers.

"Houses" from UP THE WINDY HILL by Aileen Fisher. Copyright © 1953 by Abelard Press. © renewed 1981 by Aileen Fisher. Reprinted by permission of Marian Reiner for the author.

"Fog" from CHICAGO POEMS by Carl Sandburg, copyright 1916 by Holt, Rinehart and Winston and renewed 1944 by Carl Sandburg, reprinted by permission of Harcourt, Inc.

"The Cat Who Became a Poet" reprinted with the permission of Margaret K. McElderry Books, an imprint of Simon & Schuster Children's Publishing Division from NONSTOP NONSENSE by Margaret Mahy, illustrated by Quentin Blake. Text copyright © 1977 Margaret Mahy. Illustrations copyright © 1977 by Quentin Blake. "The Cat Who Became a Poet" from NONSTOP NONSENSE by Margaret Mahy, text copyright (c) 1977 Margaret Mahy, Victor Gollancz, publisher. Used by permission of The Orion Publishing Group Ltd.

From A CLOAK FOR THE DREAMER by Aileen Friedman, illustrated by Kim Howard. A Marilyn Burns Brainy Day Book. Copyright © 1994 by Marilyn Burns Education Associates. Reprinted by permission of Scholastic Inc.

"Picasso" from Getting to Know the World's Greatest Artists: PICASSO by Mike Venezia, copyright © 1988 by Mike Venezia. All rights reserved. Reprinted by permission of Children's Press an imprint of Scholastic Library Publishing, Inc.

From THE EMPEROR'S NEW CLOTHES by Nadine Bernard Westcott. Copyright © 1984 by Nadine Bernard Westcott. By permission of Little, Brown and Company (Inc.).

ROXABOXEN by Alice McLerran. TEXT COPYRIGHT © 1991 BY ALICE MCLERRAN. ILLUSTRATIONS COPYRIGHT © 1991 BY BARBARA COONEY. Used by permission of HarperCollins Publishers.

"The Sun is a Yellow-Tipped Porcupine", from WHIRLWIND IS A GHOST DANCING by Natalia Belting, copyright © 1974 by Natalia Belting. Used by permission of Dutton Children's Books, an imprint of Penguin Putnam Books for Young Readers, a division of Penguin Putnam Inc.

www.sra4kids.com

SRA/McGraw-Hill

A Division of The McGraw-Hill Companies

Send all inquiries to:
SRA/McGraw-Hill
8787 Orion Place
Columbus, OH 43240-4027

Printed in the United States of America.

ISBN 0-07-602694-9

3 4 5 6 7 8 9 RRW 10 09 08 07 06 05

— PROGRAM AUTHORS —

Marilyn Jager Adams, Ph.D.
BBN Technologies

Carl Bereiter, Ph.D.
University of Toronto

Joe Campione, Ph.D.
University of California, Berkeley

Iva Carruthers, Ph.D.
Northeastern Illinois University

Jan Hirshberg, Ed.D.
Reading Specialist

Anne McKeough, Ph.D.
University of Calgary

Michael Pressley, Ph.D.
Michigan State University

Marsha Roit, Ph.D.
National Reading Consultant

Marlene Scardamalia, Ph.D.
University of Toronto

Gerald H. Treadway, Jr., Ed.D.
San Diego State University

Marcy Stein, Ph.D.
University of Washington, Tacoma

Table of Contents
Friendship

Friendship 12

Gloria Who Might Be My Best Friend 14
*from **The Stories Julian Tells***
realistic fiction by Ann Cameron
illustrated by Ann Strugnell
Concept Connections 26
Meet the Author, Ann Cameron
Meet the Illustrator, Ann Strugnell 27
🏅 *Irma Simonton Black Award*

Angel Child, Dragon Child 28
realistic fiction by Michele Maria Surat
illustrated by Vo-Dinh Mai
Concept Connections 44
Meet the Author, Michele Maria Surat
Meet the Illustrator, Vo-Dinh Mai 45
🏅 *ALA Booklist Editor's Choice*

Janey 46
a poem by Charlotte Zolotow
illustrated by Leah Palmer Preiss

The Tree House 48
realistic fiction by Lois Lowry
illustrated by Trina Schart Hyman
Concept Connections 60
Meet the Author, Lois Lowry
Meet the Illustrator, Trina Schart Hyman 61

Fine Art 62

Conjunction. Romare Bearden
Children Had Few Toys. William Barnhill
The Good Friends. Honoré Daumier

Rugby & Rosie 64

*realistic fiction written
and illustrated by* Nan Parson Rossiter

Concept Connections 80

Meet the Author/Illustrator, Nan Parson Rossiter 81

American Bookseller "Pick of the Lists"

Teammates 82

a biography by Peter Golenbock
illustrated by Paul Bacon

Concept Connections 92

Meet the Author, Peter Golenbock

Meet the Illustrator, Paul Bacon 93

Notable Children's Trade Book (Social Studies)

The Legend of Damon and Pythias 94

a myth adapted as a play by Fan Kissen
illustrated by Fabricio Vanden Broeck

Concept Connections 110

Meet the Author, Fan Kissen

Meet the Illustrator, Fabricio Vanden Broeck 111

Table of Contents

City Wildlife 112

The Boy Who Didn't Believe in Spring 114
realistic fiction by Lucille Clifton
illustrated by Brinton Turkle
Concept Connections 124
Meet the Author, Lucille Clifton
Meet the Illustrator, Brinton Turkle 125

City Critters: Wild Animals Live in Cities, Too . . . 126
from *3-2-1 Contact* magazine
an expository text by Richard Chevat
Concept Connections 132
Meet the Author, Richard Chevat 133

Raccoon 134
a poem by Mary Ann Hoberman
illustrated by Pamela Carroll

Make Way for Ducklings 136
a fantasy written and illustrated by Robert McCloskey
Concept Connections 144
Meet the Author/Illustrator, Robert McCloskey 145
Caldecott Medal

Fine Art 146
Lunch in the Gardens. Beryl Cook
Cable Car Festival. Dong Kingman

Urban Roosts: Where Birds Nest in the City ...148

from the book of the same title
an expository text by Barbara Bash

Concept Connections 162

Meet the Author/Illustrator, Barbara Bash 163
  Outstanding Science Trade Book Award

The Worm 164

a poem by Raymond Souster
illustrated by Robert Byrd

Pigeons 165

a poem by Lilian Moore
illustrated by Robert Byrd

Two Days in May 166

realistic fiction by Harriet Peck Taylor
illustrated by Leyla Torres

Concept Connections 180

Meet the Author, Harriet Peck Taylor

Meet the Illustrator, Leyla Torres 181
  Parent's Choice Recommendation

Secret Place 182

realistic fiction by Eve Bunting
illustrated by Ted Rand

Concept Connections 194

Meet the Author, Eve Bunting

Meet the Illustrator, Ted Rand 195

Table of Contents
Imagination

Imagination 196

Through Grandpa's Eyes 198
realistic fiction by Patricia MacLachlan
illustrated by Deborah Kogan Ray
Concept Connections 212
Meet the Author, Patricia MacLachlan
Meet the Illustrator, Deborah Kogan Ray 213
    Notable Children's Trade Book (Social Studies)

The Apple 214
a poem by Arnold Adoff
illustrated by Deborah Drummond

Houses 215
a poem by Aileen Fisher
illustrated by Deborah Drummond

Fog 215
a poem by Carl Sandburg
illustrated by Deborah Drummond

The Cat Who Became a Poet 216
from *Nonstop Nonsense*
a fantasy by Margaret Mahy
illustrated by Quentin Blake
Concept Connections 222
Meet the Author, Margaret Mahy
Meet the Illustrator, Quentin Blake 223
    Parenting's Reading Magic Award

    Hans Christian Andersen Award for Illustration

A Cloak for the Dreamer 224
realistic fiction by Aileen Friedman
illustrated by Kim Howard
Concept Connections 236
Meet the Author, Aileen Friedman
Meet the Illustrator, Kim Howard .237

Fine Art 238
Cow Triptych. Roy Lichtenstein
Time Transfixed. René Magritte
The Desk. David Hockney
Baird Trogon. Robert Lostutter

Picasso 240
from the book **Picasso**
a biography by Mike Venezia
Concept Connections 248
Meet the Author, Mike Venezia .249

The Emperor's New Clothes 250
a fairy tale by Hans Christian Andersen
retold and illustrated by Nadine Bernard Westcott
Concept Connections 258
Meet the Author, Hans Christian Andersen
Meet the Author/Illustrator,
Nadine Bernard Westcott 259
Redbook Children's Picturebook Award

Roxaboxen 260
realistic fiction by Alice McLerran
illustrated by Barbara Cooney
Concept Connections 268
Meet the Author, Alice McLerran
Meet the Illustrator, Barbara Cooney 269
Southwest Book Award

The sun is a yellow-tipped porcupine 270
a Crow Indian poem
illustrated by Tricia Courtney

Glossary 272

Friendship

Friendship can be confusing, nice, sad, and very, very important. What is a friend? How do you become a friend? What can you expect of a friend? Everyone has these questions, but what are the answers?

Gloria Who Might Be My Best Friend

from ***The Stories Julian Tells***
by Ann Cameron
illustrated by Ann Strugnell

If you have a girl for a friend, people find out and tease you. That's why I didn't want a girl for a friend—not until this summer, when I met Gloria.

It happened one afternoon when I was walking down the street by myself. My mother was visiting a friend of hers, and Huey was visiting a friend of his. Huey's friend is five and so I think he is too young to play with. And there aren't any kids just my age. I was walking down the street feeling lonely.

A block from our house I saw a moving van in front of a brown house, and men were carrying in chairs and tables and bookcases and boxes full of I don't know what. I watched for a while, and suddenly I heard a voice right behind me.

"Who are you?"

I turned around and there was a girl in a yellow dress. She looked the same age as me. She had curly hair that was braided into two pigtails with red ribbons at the ends.

"I'm Julian," I said. "Who are you?"

"I'm Gloria," she said. "I come from Newport. Do you know where Newport is?"

I wasn't sure, but I didn't tell Gloria. "It's a town on the ocean," I said.

"Right," Gloria said. "Can you turn a cartwheel?"

She turned sideways herself and did two cartwheels on the grass.

I had never tried a cartwheel before, but I tried to copy Gloria. My hands went down in the grass, my feet went up in the air, and—I fell over.

I looked at Gloria to see if she was laughing at me. If she was laughing at me, I was going to go home and forget about her.

But she just looked at me very seriously and said, "It takes practice," and then I liked her.

"I know where there's a bird's nest in your yard," I said.

"Really?" Gloria said. "There weren't any trees in the yard, or any birds, where I lived before."

I showed her where a robin lives and has eggs. Gloria stood up on a branch and looked in. The eggs were small and pale blue. The mother robin squawked at us, and she and the father robin flew around our heads.

"They want us to go away," Gloria said. She got down from the branch, and we went around to the front of the house and watched the moving men carry two rugs and a mirror inside.

"Would you like to come over to my house?" I said.

"All right," Gloria said, "if it is all right with my mother." She ran in the house and asked.

It was all right, so Gloria and I went to my house, and I showed her my room and my games and my rock collection, and then I made strawberry Kool-Aid and we sat at the kitchen table and drank it.

"You have a red mustache on your mouth," Gloria said.

"You have a red mustache on your mouth, too," I said.

Gloria giggled, and we licked off the mustaches with our tongues.

"I wish you'd live here a long time," I told Gloria.

Gloria said, "I wish I would too.

"I know the best way to make wishes," Gloria said.

"What's that?" I asked.

"First you make a kite. Do you know how to make one?"

"Yes," I said, "I know how." I know how to make good kites because my father taught me. We make them out of two crossed sticks and folded newspaper.

"All right," Gloria said, "that's the first part of making wishes that come true. So let's make a kite."

We went out into the garage and spread out sticks and newspaper and made a kite. I fastened on the kite string and went to the closet and got rags for the tail.

"Do you have some paper and two pencils?" Gloria asked. "Because now we make the wishes."

I didn't know what she was planning, but I went in the house and got pencils and paper.

"All right," Gloria said. "Every wish you want to have come true you write on a long thin piece of paper. You don't tell me your wishes, and I don't tell you mine. If you tell, your wishes don't come true. Also, if you look at the other person's wishes, your wishes don't come true."

Gloria sat down on the garage floor again and started writing her wishes. I wanted to see what they were—but I went to the other side of the garage and wrote my own wishes instead. I wrote:

1. I wish the fig tree would be the tallest in town.
2. I wish I'd be a great soccer player.
3. I wish I could ride in an airplane.
4. I wish Gloria would stay here and be my best friend.

I folded my four wishes in my fist and went over to Gloria.

"How many wishes did you make?" Gloria asked.

"Four," I said. "How many did you make?"

"Two," Gloria said.

I wondered what they were.

"Now we put the wishes on the tail of the kite," Gloria said. "Every time we tie one piece of rag on the tail, we fasten a wish in the knot. You can put yours in first."

I fastened mine in, and then Gloria fastened in hers, and we carried the kite into the yard.

"You hold the tail," I told Gloria, "and I'll pull."

We ran through the back yard with the kite, passed the garden and the fig tree, and went into the open field beyond our yard.

The kite started to rise. The tail jerked heavily like a long white snake. In a minute the kite passed the roof of my house and was climbing toward the sun.

We stood in the open field, looking up at it. I was wishing I would get my wishes.

"I know it's going to work!" Gloria said.

"How do you know?"

"When we take the kite down," Gloria told me, "there shouldn't be one wish in the tail. When the wind takes all your wishes, that's when you know it's going to work."

The kite stayed up for a long time. We both held the string. The kite looked like a tiny black spot in the sun, and my neck got stiff from looking at it.

"Shall we pull it in?" I asked.

"All right," Gloria said.

We drew the string in more and more until, like a tired bird, the kite fell at our feet.

We looked at the tail. All our wishes were gone. Probably they were still flying higher and higher in the wind.

Maybe I would get to be a good soccer player and have a ride in an airplane and the tallest fig tree in town. And Gloria would be my best friend.

"Gloria," I said, "did you wish we would be friends?"

"You're not supposed to ask me that!" Gloria said.

"I'm sorry," I answered. But inside I was smiling. I guessed one thing Gloria wished for. I was pretty sure we would be friends.

Gloria
Who Might Be
My Best Friend

Concept Connections
Linking the Selection

Think about the following questions, and then record your responses in the Response Journal section of your Writer's Notebook.

• Do you think it was hard for Julian to ask Gloria to be his friend? Why?

• How did the kite help Julian and Gloria become friends?

Exploring Concept Vocabulary

The concept word for this lesson is **kindness.** If you do not know what this word means, look it up in a dictionary. Answer these questions:

• How did Gloria first show **kindness** toward Julian?

• Why was Gloria's first show of **kindness** toward Julian important to their friendship?

In the Vocabulary section of your Writer's Notebook, write a sentence using the word **kindness** and one of the selection vocabulary words.

Expanding the Concept

Think about the story "Gloria Who Might Be My Best Friend." What did you learn about friendship from this story?

Try to use the word **kindness** in your discussion. Add new ideas about friendship to the Concept/Question Board.

Meet the Author

Ann Cameron was in third grade when she knew she wanted to be a writer. It has been the memories of her friends and the stories they have shared that help her write stories. She says, *"My story will never be exactly like yours. I could never tell yours for you. Your story, if it's really the way you want to tell it, can never be wrong the way an arithmetic answer is wrong; and even if your mother, your father, your teacher, or your best friend doesn't understand it, it's still right for you . . . stories are individual, special, and all different—brand-new thought-flowers blooming in the garden of your head."*

Ann now lives in Guatemala, where the neighborhood children continue to inspire her writing. She is also the supervisor of a local library, where she loves to watch children read and learn.

Meet the Illustrator

Ann Strugnell is a British artist who has illustrated many children's books. She has traveled to faraway places such as Turkey, Spain, and Italy. She has even been to the United States to see New York and Cape Cod. She lives with her husband and illustrates books in the bustling city of London, England. Sometimes she comes to the United States to illustrate books as well.

Focus Questions What might it be like to be in a new school and in a new country? How would you make friends if you didn't speak the same language as the rest of your classmates?

Angel Child, Dragon Child

Michele Maria Surat
illustrated by Vo-Dinh Mai

My sisters skipped through the stone gate two by two. Mother was not there to skip with me. Mother was far away in Vietnam. She could not say, "Ut, my little one, be an Angel Child. Be happy in your new American school."

I hugged the wall and peeked around the corner.

A boy with fire-colored hair pointed his finger. "Pajamas!" he shouted. "They wore white pajamas to school!" The American children tilted back their long noses, laughing.

I turned away. "I want to go home to Father and Little Quang," I said.

Chi Hai's hands curved over my shoulders. "Children stay where parents place them, Ut. We stay."

Somewhere, a loud bell jangled. I lost my sisters in a swirl of rushing children. "Pa-jaa-mas!" they teased.

Inside, the children did not sit together and chant as I was taught. Instead, they waved their hands and said their lessons one by one. I hid my hands, but the teacher called my name. "Nguyen Hoa."

Hoa is my true name, but I am Ut. Ut is my at-home name——a tender name for smallest daughter.

"Hoa," the teacher said slowly. "Write your name, please." She pressed a chalk-piece to my hand and wrote in the air.

"I not understand," I whispered. The round-eyed children twittered. The red-haired boy poked my back.

"Stand up, Pajamas!"

I stood and bowed. "*Chao buoi sang*,"
I said like an Angel Child. The children
screeched like bluejays.

I sat down and flipped up my desk top, hiding
my angry Dragon face.

Deep in my pocket, I felt Mother's gift—a small
wooden matchbox with silvery edges. I took it out
and traced the *hoa-phuong* on the lid. When I
tapped the tiny drawer, Mother's eyes peeked over
the edge.

"I will keep you safe in here, Mother," I told her.
"See? You will just fit beside the crayons."

Her listening face smiled. In my heart, I heard
the music of her voice. "Do not be angry, my
smallest daughter," she said. "Be my brave little
Dragon."

So all day I was brave, even when the children
whispered behind their hands and the clock
needles ticked slowly. Finally, the bell trilled.
Time for home!

As soon as he saw me, Little Quang crowed, "Ut!
Ut! Ut!" His laughing eyes gleamed like watermelon
seeds. I dropped my books and slung him on
my hip.

There he rode, tugging my hair as I sorted
mint leaves and chives. Little Quang strung rice
noodles from the cup hooks. Father and I laughed
at this happy play.

At night, small brother curled tight beside me.
I showed him Mother's lonely face inside the
matchbox. Together we prayed, "Keep Mother
safe. Send her to us soon." With Mother's picture
near, we slept like Angel Children.

In this way, many days passed.

One day at school, small feathers floated past the frosty windows. "Mother," I whispered, "this is snow. It makes everything soft, even the angry trees with no leaves to make them pretty."

My fingers danced on the desk top while I waited for the bell. When it rang, I rushed out the door.

Outside, snowflakes left wet kisses on my cheeks. "Chi Hai!" I called. "Catch some!"

"It disappears!" she cried.

Just as Chi Hai spoke, a snowrock stung her chin. That red-haired boy darted behind the dumpster. He was laughing hard.

I tried, but I could not be a noble Dragon. Before I knew it, I was scooping up snow. My hands burned and my fingers turned red. I threw my snowrock and the laughing stopped.

Suddenly, the boy tackled me! We rolled in the snow, kicking and yelling, until the principal's large hand pinched my shoulder.

"Inside!" he thundered, and he marched us to our classroom.

"We can't have this fighting. You two have to help each other," ordered the principal. He pointed at me. "Hoa, you need to speak to Raymond. Use our words. Tell him about Vietnam." Raymond glared. "And you, Raymond, you must learn to listen. You will write Hoa's story."

"But I can't understand her funny words," Raymond whined. "Anyway, I don't have a pencil."

"Use this one, then," said the principal. He slapped down a pencil, turned and slammed the door. His shoes squeegeed down the hall.

"Pajamas!" Raymond hissed. He crinkled his paper and snapped the pencil in two. He hid his head in his arms. How could I tell my story to *him*?

The clock needles blurred before my eyes. No! I *would not* be an Angel Child for this cruel-hearted boy.

But later, across the room, I heard a sniffle. Raymond's shoulders jiggled like Little Quang's when he cried for Mother.

I crept over. Gently, I tugged the sad boy's sleeve. He didn't move. "Raymond," I pleaded, "not cry. I give you cookie."

Suddenly, his head bounced up. "Hoa!" he shouted. "You said my name. You didn't use funny words." He broke off a piece of the cookie.

"I say English," I answered proudly. "And you call me Ut. Ut is my at-home name, from Vietnam."

"Okay, *Ut*," he mumbled. "But only if you tell me what's in your matchbox."

"My mother," I told him. We giggled and ate the cookie crumbs.

Then Raymond asked, "Why do you need your mother's picture?"

"Mother is far away," I said softly.

"She didn't come with you?"

"So many children in my family," I sighed. "No money for Mother to come."

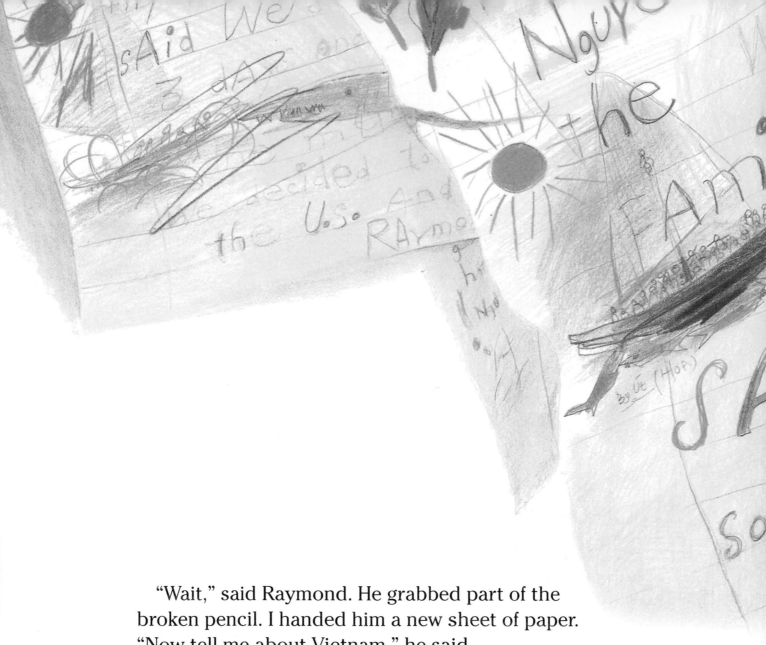

"Wait," said Raymond. He grabbed part of the broken pencil. I handed him a new sheet of paper. "Now tell me about Vietnam," he said.

Raymond scrawled my words in black squiggles. I crayoned pictures in the margins.

When we were ready, Raymond leaned out the door. "Done!" he beamed. He waved the story like a flag.

The principal squeegeed up the hall. "You may go," said the big man.

We dashed through the stone gate together.

The next day, the principal read our story to the whole school. "These girls sailed many oceans to be here. They left behind their home, their friends, and most important of all, their mother. So now . . ."

"Ut's mother needs money for the long boat ride to America!" shouted a familiar voice. Raymond stood on his chair. "And we could have a fair and *earn* the money."

"Young man!" warned the principal.

Raymond slid down in his seat. "We could," he insisted. I hid my eyes. I held my breath. Chi Hai squeezed my hand.

"A special fair! A Vietnamese fair!" my teacher exclaimed. My eyes opened wide.

The principal's eyebrows wiggled like caterpillars. "But who will help with a Vietnamese fair?"

"Me!" cried Raymond.

"We will!" squealed the children.

"Well, what are we waiting for?" said the principal. And we all clapped for the fair.

On the special day, I wore my white *ao dai* and welcomed everyone to our Vietnamese fair. "*Chao buoi sang,*" I said, bowing like an Angel Child.

"*Chao buoi sang,*" they answered, smiling.

High above our heads, our rainbow dragon floated freely. Below, Chi Hai and her friends sold rice cakes, imperial rolls and sesame cookies. Raymond popped balloons and won three goldfish. He gave one to Little Quang. "Don't eat it," he warned.

By the end of the day, we had just enough money to send to Mother. "When will she come?" I wondered.

Every day, we walked home wondering, "When will Mother come?"

We slid through icy winter. . . .

We splish-splashed through spring rain. . . .

We tiptoed barefoot through the grass, still hoping she would come.

On the last day of school, when I knew the *hoa-phuong* were blossoming in Vietnam, Raymond and I raced home faster than all my sisters. We were the first to see Father and Little Quang at the picture window, and beside them . . .

Mother!

Angel Child, Dragon Child

Concept Connections

Linking the Selection

Think about the following questions, and then record your responses in the Response Journal section of your Writer's Notebook.

- How did Ut's mother's gift help Ut when she was at school without any friends?

- How did Ut and Raymond become friends?

- What did Raymond do to show his friendship for Ut?

Exploring Concept Vocabulary

The concept word for this lesson is *communicate.* If you do not know what this word means, look it up in a dictionary. Answer these questions:

- How did Ut and Raymond *communicate* kindness toward one another?

- How did learning to *communicate* with each other help Ut and Raymond become friends?

In the Vocabulary section of your Writer's Notebook, write a sentence using the word *communicate* and one of the selection vocabulary words.

Expanding the Concept

Think about Julian and Gloria's friendship in "Gloria Who Might Be My Best Friend" and Ut and Raymond's friendship. Compare how the characters became friends and how they showed their friendship toward each other.

Try to use the word **communicate** in your discussion.

Add new ideas about friendship to the Concept/Question Board.

Meet the Author

Michele Maria Surat teaches high school near Washington, D.C., when she is not writing. The tale of Ut, the main character in this story, began when a Vietnamese student came to Surat with tear-filled eyes and shared a photograph of her mother in Vietnam. Surat wanted to tell the story of the brave students she worked with in hopes of creating an understanding between Vietnamese and American children.

Meet the Illustrator

Vo-Dinh Mai is an artist and author from Vietnam. He came to the United States when he was twenty-seven years old. Before that he spent time studying art in Paris, France. In addition to painting, Vo-Dinh loves printmaking from woodcuts. He also loves illustrating books and says, *"I believe that good illustrations can enrich the mind of a reader, young or old...."*

Vo-Dinh was back in Vietnam during the Vietnam War. He has this to say about how the war affects his art: *"If anything, the war between Vietnamese and between Vietnamese and Americans has reinforced my faith in the miracle of life."*

Janey

Charlotte Zolotow
illustrated by Leah Palmer Preiss

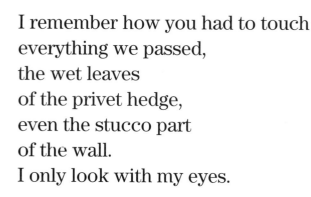

Janey
it's lonely
all day long
since you moved away.

When I walk in the rain
and the leaves are wet
and clinging to the sidewalk
I remember
how we used to walk
home from school
together.

I remember how you had to touch
everything we passed,
the wet leaves
of the privet hedge,
even the stucco part
of the wall.
I only look with my eyes.

I still have the pebble
you found on the
playground.
And I remember how
you skipped flat rocks
into the pond.
Mine just sank.

46

Sometimes when I'm playing
with the other kids
I remember how your voice sounded.
No one else sounds like you.

I remember sometimes
we both talked at once
and when we stopped
we'd said the same thing.
And I remember sitting on the steps
in the sun and not talking
at all.
There is no one else
I can sit with
and not talk.

I remember how
we'd go home for dinner
and I could hardly wait
for dinner to end
to call you.
But sometimes you called me first.

And I remember last Christmas
I half didn't want
to give you your present,
I wanted it so much myself.

You told me later
you half didn't want to give me mine
but when we each opened our present
it was the *same* book.
I think of you every time
I read the stories over again.

When the wind blows
through the trees at night
I remember how we used to
listen together
nights you slept over.

I didn't want you to move away.
You didn't want to either.
Janey
maybe some day
we'll grow up
and live near each other
again.

I wish you hadn't moved away.

The Tree House

Lois Lowry
illustrated by Trina Schart Hyman

t was a terrific tree house. *Better* than terrific: It was a marvelous, magnificent, one-of-a-kind tree house, with wooden walls painted bright blue. It had two windows, with red shutters on each, and a yellow door with two shiny brass hinges and a small brass bell that rang when you pulled a string. There was a little porch where you could sit with your legs dangling.

Inside were a table, a chair, a small rug with fringe on each end, and two fat pillows so that you could lie on the rug and read.

You reached it by climbing a ladder—a ladder to the best tree house ever. And it belonged to Chrissy.

48

"It's all mine, isn't it?" she had asked her grandfather after he built the house for her. "Just mine, and nobody else's?"

Grandpa was washing his paintbrush. He nodded. "I built it just for you," he said.

So Chrissy used her markers and made a sign. CHRISSY'S HOUSE, the sign said. KEEP OUT! She tacked it to the door. Then she took her favorite books into the tree house, curled up on the pillows, and began to read.

"Chrissy?" The voice came from the next yard, from just across the fence.

Chrissy got up and looked through the tree house window. "Hi, Leah," she said to the girl who lived next door. "How do you like my tree house, now that it's all done?"

"It's beautiful," Leah said. "What do you have inside?"

"A table and two chairs and a rug and some pillows," Chrissy told her. "And some secret stuff," she added, though she didn't have secret stuff, really. She *planned* to.

"Can I come up and see?" Leah asked.

"No," Chrissy said. "It's just for me. That's why I made the sign."

Leah stood silently for a moment. Then she said, "I hate you, Chrissy."

"I hate you, too," Chrissy replied. She went back to the pillows and opened her book again.

A short time later, she heard voices in the next yard. She peered through her window and saw that Leah's father was there with Leah. They had a wheelbarrow full of old boards, and a jar of nails. As Chrissy watched from her window, she saw Leah's father prop an old ladder against the trunk of the tree on the other side of the fence. Then, after he jiggled the ladder and made certain it was steady, he climbed up, carrying a board, and began to nail it into place where the branches came together.

He was making Leah a tree house. Chrissy laughed to herself. Leah's father was at home because he had lost his job. She knew they didn't have extra money now for things like paint and brass hinges. And Leah's tree house would never be as good as hers. Never in a million years. Chrissy went back to her book and turned the pages while the hammering continued.

That evening, after supper, Chrissy stood beside the fence and looked up at Leah's finished house. She laughed aloud.

It had taken a week for Grandpa to finish building her beautiful tree house. Grandpa had used new wooden boards from the lumberyard. But Leah's had been completed in a day, and Chrissy could see that it was made from the stack of old weathered boards that had been in the corner of Leah's yard. Only one board remained there now; the others had become the tree house.

The house had walls and a porch and a door and two windows, but it had no shutters and no paint and no door bell. The boards were crooked, and the roof had holes where the pieces of wood didn't quite meet.

Even the sign wasn't as good, because Leah had done hers with crayons instead of marking pens. But its message was the same. LEAH'S HOUSE, it said. KEEP OUT.

Leah's head appeared in the window of her tree house.

"Your house is not as nice as mine," Chrissy told her.

"Not on the outside," Leah said. "But inside, it's better."

Chrissy wondered what Leah had inside her tree house. But she didn't ask.

For several days the two girls didn't speak to each other. They sat alone in their tree houses. By the fourth day, Chrissy had finished all her books and had read some of them twice. She went to her window and called across the fence to Leah.

"Do you have any books I can borrow?" she asked, when Leah's head appeared.

"No. Our car's broken so we can't go to the library."

"You don't have any books at *all?*"

Leah shook her head.

Chrissy sat back down. She wondered what it would be like to be in a tree house with no books at all. She wondered what Leah was doing in there.

Finally she called across the fence again. "Would you like to borrow some of mine?" she asked. And Leah said yes.

So Chrissy climbed down, stood at the fence, and handed two books over to Leah, who had climbed down her ladder, too.

"I have some bananas," Leah told her. "Do you want one?" Chrissy nodded, and Leah climbed up and returned with a banana to pass across the fence.

Back in her own tree house, Chrissy peeled and ate the banana. Then she called to Leah again.

"Do you have a wastebasket in your house? I don't want to mess up my carpeting with this banana peel."

Leah, looking through her window, nodded. So Chrissy climbed down, and Leah climbed down, and Chrissy handed the banana peel across the fence.

Both girls climbed back into their houses. Chrissy sat alone and admired her fringed rug for a moment, then leafed through her books again, wondering what Leah was doing. She called through her window.

"Leah?"

Leah looked out. "What?"

"I could come visit you if you want," Chrissy said.

Leah didn't answer.

"Or you could come visit me," Chrissy added.

"Your sign says KEEP OUT," Leah pointed out.

"So does mine."

"Well," Chrissy suggested, "we could change them."

Leah nodded. Each girl removed her sign and crossed out the words KEEP OUT. They wrote WELCOME instead. They rehung their signs.

"You know what, Chrissy?" Leah said. "We could use that wide board in the corner of my yard. It would go from your porch to my porch, over the top of the fence. Then we could visit each other by walking across the board."

Chrissy eyed the distance and the height. "What if we fell?"

"It's not very high," Leah pointed out. "And if we each came out halfway and held hands, we could help each other across."

They climbed down their ladders. The wide board was heavy, but when each girl took an end they were able to lift it into place. In a few minutes they had made a bridge between the houses, over the top of the fence.

Chrissy stepped from her tree house porch onto the wide board, reached for Leah's waiting hand, and walked across. She entered Leah's tree house and looked around.

There was no rug, and the only books were her own that Leah had borrowed. But there was a bowl of fruit, a wastebasket, and curtains at the windows. The walls were covered with portraits of beautiful women—the most beautiful women Chrissy had ever seen.

"I like your art collection, Leah," Chrissy said.

"They're left over from where my mom works," Leah explained. "She works at a beauty parlor, and they get pictures of all the new hairstyles. These are last year's."

"You can't tell. They look brand new."

"My house isn't as nice as yours," Leah added. "I said it was better inside, but it isn't, really."

"I don't really have carpeting," Chrissy admitted. "Only an old rug. And I don't have curtains, or a single picture on my walls."

"I could let you have one of my pictures. Two, even. You can have the blonde shag and the auburn blunt cut."

"My grandpa had paint left over. He could paint the outside of your house so we'd match. But I'm afraid we don't have another door bell."

"Now that my sign says WELCOME, I don't think I need a door bell," Leah said.

"I don't really hate you, Leah," Chrissy said.

"I don't really hate you, either," Leah replied.

They sat together on Leah's porch and looked around happily.

"What do you think is the best part of a tree house, Chrissy?" Leah asked.

Chrissy thought. She looked over at her own house, with its shutters and brass hinges. She looked around at Leah's, with its bowl of bright apples and its yellow curtains.

"The *very* best part," she said finally, "is the bridge."

The Tree House

Concept Connections
Linking the Selection

Think about the following questions, and then record your responses in the Response Journal section of your Writer's Notebook.

- How did Chrissy's tree house hurt her friendship with Leah?

- Why did Chrissy and Leah decide to change their signs from **KEEP OUT** to **WELCOME?**

Exploring Concept Vocabulary

The concept word for this lesson is *thoughtfulness.* If you do not know what this word means, look it up in a dictionary. Answer these questions:

- What does *thoughtfulness* have to do with being a friend?

- How did Chrissy show *thoughtfulness* in the story? How did Leah show *thoughtfulness?*

In the Vocabulary section of your Writer's Notebook, write a sentence using the word *thoughtfulness* and one of the selection vocabulary words.

Expanding the Concept

Think about the main characters in "The Tree House." What did they help you learn about friendship?

Try to use the word *thoughtfulness* in your discussion of the characters.

Add new ideas about friendship to the Concept/Question Board.

Meet the Author

Lois Lowry was born in Honolulu, Hawaii. Her father was in the army, so the family lived in many different places. She even attended junior high school in Tokyo, Japan. Lowry taught herself to read before she was four years old when she realized that letters made sounds, sounds made words, words made sentences, and sentences made stories. She was so excited by her discovery that she says, *"It was then that I decided that one day I would write books."* She wrote her first children's book when she was forty years old, in honor of her sister Helen who died of cancer. Since then she has published many children's stories, some of them based upon the lives of her own children.

Meet the Illustrator

Trina Schart Hyman worked many years before she became a famous children's illustrator. She started drawing when she was young and went on to art schools in her hometown of Philadelphia, Pennsylvania. While living in Sweden, she got her first job illustrating *Pippi Longstocking*. It took her only two weeks. She later returned to the United States and had many rejections before getting work as an illustrator. In 1985 she won a Caldecott Award, one of the most important awards for children's books, for *Saint George and the Dragon*. Trina Schart Hyman is known for using people from her life, including her neighbors, friends, their children, and her children, in her illustrations.

Conjunction. 1971. **Romare Bearden.** Piquette. ©Romare
Bearden Foundation/Licensed by VAGA, New York, NY.

Children Had Few Toys. c. 1914–17.
William Barnhill. Silver gelatin print.
Library of Congress.

**The Good
Friends.** c. 1864.
Honoré Daumier.
Pen, brush and ink,
conte crayon,
watercolor, and
charcoal on wove
paper. 236 × 303
mm. The Baltimore
Museum of Art.

Rugby & Rosie

by Nan Parson Rossiter

Rugby is my dog. He is a chocolate Labrador, and we have had him for as long as I can remember.

He walks with me to the school-bus stop in the morning, and he meets me there when I get home. He follows me around when I do my chores, and he sleeps beside my bed at night. He is my best friend.

We used to do everything together—just the two of us.

Then Rosie came.

One fall day, my dad brought home a little yellow puppy. Her name was Rosie. She was so cute that I loved her right away. But she wasn't an ordinary puppy. She was coming to live with my family for only a year.

Then Rosie would be old enough to go to a special school. There she would learn how to be a guide dog for a blind person. She and her new owner would always be together. They would be best friends. Just like Rugby and me.

I knew all this before Rosie came, but Rugby didn't.
I held the puppy out to him to see how he would greet
Rosie. She leaned forward eagerly and licked Rugby
right on the nose.

Rugby gave one sniff and turned away. He made it
very clear he wasn't interested in being friends.

"Come on, Rugby," I said. "She wants to play with
you." And it was true. Rosie did want to play. But
Rugby wasn't in the mood.

My mom and dad told me to be patient with Rugby,
that he'd get used to having another dog around the
house. But I wasn't sure. He looked so sad. Maybe he
thought I didn't love him anymore, which wasn't true!

Rosie fit in with the family right away. She was so friendly and always wanted to play. She would chase after anything and then run back. She loved everyone in the family—even Rugby! But he still wasn't friendly. Day after day, Rugby just moped around and wouldn't play with us.

That didn't bother Rosie one bit. She thought Rugby was the greatest. She trotted along after him, ran between his legs, tripped him, jumped on him, and barked at him.

Rugby did his best to ignore her.

But Rosie just wouldn't give up.

Then one day, Rugby was not waiting at the school-
bus stop. I was worried. He *always* met me at the bus
stop.

I ran home—and there I found Rugby asleep on the
porch. Curled up in a little ball next to him was Rosie.
"Rugby!" I said. They both looked up at me and
wagged their tails. Rosie yawned and stretched and
settled back down against Rugby's side.

From then on, Rugby and Rosie were always together.
They romped and played and chased the falling leaves.
And they *both* waited for me at the bus stop.

69

Rosie was getting bigger. But she was still a puppy with lots of energy. Poor old Rugby tried his best to keep up! Soon winter came, and the three of us were racing and chasing through the new snow. We had so much fun together!

Sometimes it felt as if Rosie had always been with us—and always would be. I didn't want to think about the day when she would have to leave.

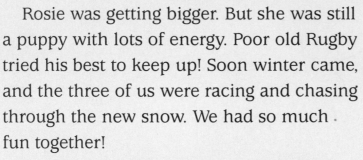

Rosie was old enough now for short lessons. Dad showed me how to teach her simple commands: *come, sit, stand, down, stay,* and *heel*.

We all worked to teach her good manners. A dog who begged for food at the table or jumped up on people would not make a good guide dog.

Rosie learned fast. Dad said that she was very smart and loved to please people. But she would have to pass many tests before she could become a guide dog.

I asked Dad what would happen if Rosie didn't pass the tests. He said that she couldn't be a guide dog, but she could still be a good pet. Then we would be able to keep her.

Now I didn't know what to think. I wanted Rosie to do well. I wanted to be proud of her. And I wanted her to help a blind person someday. I knew how important that was. But it was getting harder and harder to think of Rosie going away. And how could I explain it to Rugby? He loved Rosie as much as I did. Now the three of us were best friends.

When spring came, my family started taking Rosie on trips. We wanted her to be used to cars and buses and to the places where she would have to take her blind owner, like the bank and the store. We even took her to a restaurant. Of course, Rugby couldn't come with us. He always looked a little sad when Rosie got to go somewhere he couldn't go. And I knew he would be waiting for us when we got home.

Rosie would jump out of the car, and the two of them would race off, barking and playing and jumping. Later, they would come home in time for dinner, muddy and wet, with their tongues hanging out.

Soon summer came. The days were long and hot.
Rosie was almost full grown. She was a beautiful dog.
She and Rugby liked to sleep in the cool shade together.
Sometimes the three of us went swimming in a nearby
pond. Rugby and Rosie loved to fetch sticks and tennis
balls that I threw into the water.

It was a wonderful summer, and I wanted it to last
forever.

I knew that when fall came, it would be time for Rosie to go. When that day did come, I tried to be brave. Rugby and I stood and watched as Dad opened the car door for Rosie to jump in. Rugby wasn't upset. He didn't know that Rosie wasn't coming back. But I was so sad. I took Rugby on a long walk and tried not to think about Rosie. It was just like old times, before she came—when there were just the two of us.

When Dad came home, Rugby was waiting, his tail wagging. But, of course, Rosie wasn't in the car. Rugby looked all over for her. He whined. I wanted to explain everything, but I knew he couldn't understand. Instead, I buried my face in his neck and whispered, "She's gone, and I miss her, too."

We all missed Rosie very much, especially Rugby. Her trainers called several times. At first, I hoped that Rosie wasn't doing well. Then she could come back to live with us. But the trainers said that she was doing fine and would graduate with her new owner soon. That made me feel so mixed-up. I didn't want to think about Rosie with a new owner, but I knew how important Rosie would be to a person who needed her. Could that person love her as much as Rugby and I had?

I wanted to go to the graduation and see Rosie again. Then I had a great idea. I asked Dad if we could take Rugby, too. I knew how he'd missed Rosie—after all, they'd been best friends.

We got special permission for Rugby to go to the graduation. I could hardly wait.

At the graduation, there were lots of people and dogs. Rugby spotted Rosie right away. She was in her guide-dog harness, standing beside her new owner. She seemed so calm, and we thought she looked so proud. Rugby bounded over to her, pulling me along. The two dogs greeted each other nose to nose, tails wagging. But Rosie would not leave her owner's side. She was a working dog now with an important job to do.

Her owner talked to us for a while. She told us how grateful she was to have Rosie and what a wonderful dog she was. And she thanked us for taking good care of her while she was a puppy.

When it was time to go, we said good-bye to Rosie. Poor Rugby. On the way home in the car, I tried to make him feel better. I talked to him and patted him. I told him that her new owner loved her and would take good care of her.

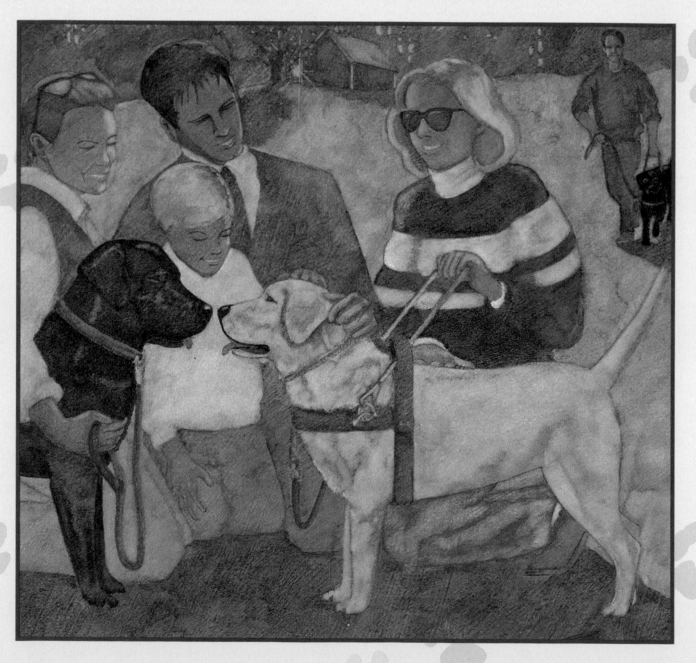

The next morning, Rugby was still moping around
when my dad left in the car. I was excited—and
nervous, too.

I knew where my dad was going.

When the car came back, I was waiting with Rugby.
Dad got out. He had a wiggly little puppy in his arms. I
knew I was holding on to Rugby too tightly—wishing,
hoping. I wanted him to know that, because we had all
loved Rosie so much, we had decided we would help
raise another puppy that would be ours for a year.

Dad knelt down in front of Rugby. "Rugby," he said,
"this is Blue."

And Rugby leaned forward and licked that little
puppy right on the nose.

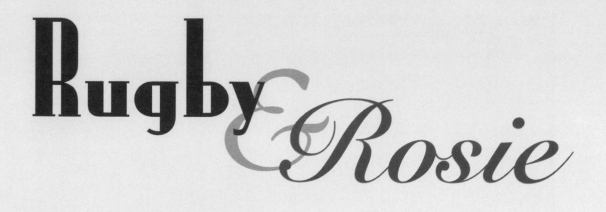

Rugby & Rosie

Concept Connections

Linking the Selection

Think about the following questions, and then record your responses in the Response Journal section of your Writer's Notebook.

- Rugby and the boy are best friends. What happened to their friendship when Rosie came to live with the family?

- Rosie left the family after only a year to learn how to be a guide dog. Why did the boy in the story sometimes wish that Rosie was not doing well with her trainers?

Exploring Concept Vocabulary

The concept word for this lesson is **affection.** If you do not know what this word means, look it up in a dictionary. Answer these questions:

- Did Rugby show **affection** toward Rosie in the beginning of the story? How do you know?

- As Rugby and Rosie developed a friendship, how did Rugby show **affection** for Rosie?

In the Vocabulary section of your Writer's Notebook, write the sentence beginning shown below. Then choose a word from the selection vocabulary, and write your own sentence ending.

The boy showed his **affection** for Rosie by _____.

Expanding the Concept

At the end of the story, Rugby is introduced to Blue, a new puppy. Do you think a friendship will develop between Rugby and Blue? Why? What do you think Rosie taught Rugby about friendship?

Try to use the word **affection** in your discussion.

Add new ideas about friendship to the Concept/Question Board.

Meet the Author and Illustrator

Nan Parson Rossiter focuses her stories on the pain of saying good-bye to loved ones. Her stories are special because the loved ones are animals. In *Rugby & Rosie* and *The Way Home*, the main characters must learn to let go of an animal that has been in their care. Rossiter never raised a guide dog, but she respects those who do. She understands the time, love, and heartbreak that is a part of such a worthwhile endeavor. Rossiter has a chocolate retriever named Briar. She lives in Connecticut with her husband and children. Each fall she loves the sad song of the Canada geese as they migrate south.

Focus Questions Why must we sometimes show courage
in order to keep a friend? Why is working together
toward a common goal important to friendships?

Teammates

Peter Golenbock
illustrated by Paul Bacon

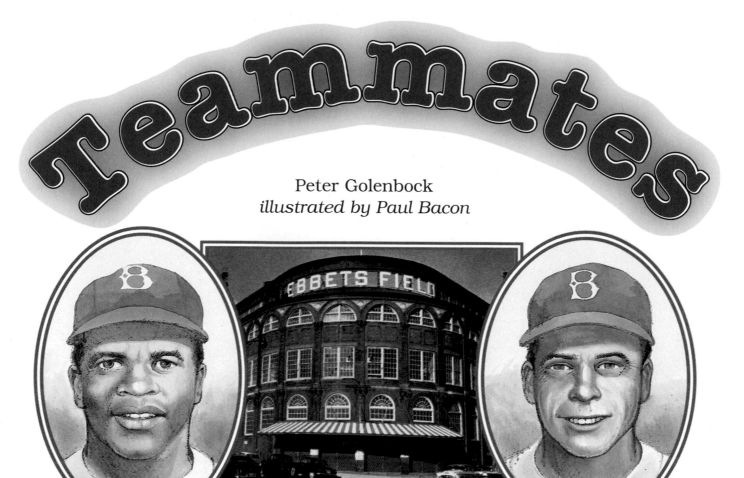

Jackie Robinson

Pee Wee Reese

Jackie Robinson was more than just my teammate.
He had a tremendous amount of talent, ability, and dedication.
Jackie set a standard for future generations of ball players.
He was a winner. Jackie Robinson was also a man.

—PEE WEE REESE
October 31, 1989

Once upon a time in America, when automobiles were black and looked like tanks and laundry was white and hung on clotheslines to dry, there were two wonderful baseball leagues that no longer exist. They were called the Negro Leagues.

The Negro Leagues had extraordinary players, and adoring fans came to see them wherever they played. They were heroes, but players in the Negro Leagues didn't make much money and their lives on the road were hard.

Laws against segregation didn't exist in the 1940s. In many places in this country, black people were not allowed to go to the same schools and churches as white people. They couldn't sit in the front of a bus or trolley car. They couldn't drink from the same drinking fountains that white people drank from.

Satchel Paige

Back then, many hotels didn't rent rooms to black people, so the Negro League players slept in their cars. Many towns had no restaurants that would serve them, so they often had to eat meals that they could buy and carry with them.

Life was very different for the players in the Major Leagues. They were the leagues for white players. Compared to the Negro League players, white players were very well paid. They stayed in good hotels and ate in fine restaurants. Their pictures were put on baseball cards and the best players became famous all over the world.

Branch Rickey

Many Americans knew that racial prejudice was wrong, but few dared to challenge openly the way things were. And many people were apathetic about racial problems. Some feared that it could be dangerous to object. Vigilante groups, like the Ku Klux Klan, reacted violently against those who tried to change the way blacks were treated.

The general manager of the Brooklyn Dodgers baseball team was a man by the name of Branch Rickey. He was not afraid of change. He wanted to treat the Dodger fans to the best players he could find, regardless of the color of their skin. He thought segregation was unfair and wanted to give everyone, regardless of race or creed, an opportunity to compete equally on ballfields across America.

To do this, the Dodgers needed one special man.

Branch Rickey launched a search for him. He was looking for a star player in the Negro Leagues who would be able to compete successfully despite threats on his life or attempts to injure him. He would have to possess the self-control not to fight back when opposing players tried to intimidate or hurt him. If this man disgraced himself on the field, Rickey knew, his opponents would use it as an excuse to keep blacks out of Major League baseball for many more years.

Rickey thought Jackie Robinson might be just the man.

Jackie rode the train to Brooklyn to meet Mr. Rickey. When Mr. Rickey told him, "I want a man with the courage not to fight back," Jackie Robinson replied, "If you take this gamble, I will do my best to perform." They shook hands. Branch Rickey and Jackie Robinson were starting on what would be known in history as "the great experiment."

Branch Rickey and Jackie Robinson.

At spring training with the Dodgers, Jackie was mobbed by blacks, young and old, as if he were a savior. He was the first black player to try out for a Major League team. If he succeeded, they knew, others would follow.

Initially, life with the Dodgers was for Jackie a series of humiliations. The players on his team who came from the South, men who had been taught to avoid black people since childhood, moved to another table whenever he sat down next to them. Many opposing players were cruel to him, calling him nasty names from their dugouts. A few tried to hurt him with their spiked shoes. Pitchers aimed at his head. And he received threats on his life, both from individuals and from organizations like the Ku Klux Klan.

Team photo of the 1947 Brooklyn Dodgers.

Despite all the difficulties, Jackie Robinson didn't give up. He made the Brooklyn Dodgers team.

But making the Dodgers was only the beginning. Jackie had to face abuse and hostility throughout the season, from April through September. His worst pain was inside. Often he felt very alone. On the road he had to live by himself, because only the white players were allowed in the hotels in towns where the team played.

The whole time Pee Wee Reese, the Dodger shortstop, was growing up in Louisville, Kentucky, he had rarely even seen a black person, unless it was in the back of a bus. Most of his friends and relatives hated the idea of his playing on the same field as a black man. In addition, Pee Wee Reese had more to lose than the other players when Jackie joined the team.

Jackie Robinson.

88

Jackie had been a shortstop, and everyone thought that Jackie would take Pee Wee's job. Lesser men might have felt anger toward Jackie, but Pee Wee was different. He told himself, "If he's good enough to take my job, he deserves it."

When his Southern teammates circulated a petition to throw Jackie off the team and asked him to sign it, Pee Wee responded, "I don't care if this man is black, blue or striped"—and refused to sign. "He can play and he can help us win," he told the others. "That's what counts."

Very early in the season, the Dodgers traveled west to Ohio to play the Cincinnati Reds. Cincinnati is near Pee Wee's hometown of Louisville.

The Reds played in a small ballpark where the fans sat close to the field. The players could almost feel the breath of the fans on the backs of their necks. Many who came that day screamed terrible, hateful things at Jackie when the Dodgers were on the field.

More than anything else, Pee Wee Reese believed in doing what was right. When he heard the fans yelling at Jackie, Pee Wee decided to take a stand.

With his head high, Pee Wee walked directly from his shortstop position to where Jackie was playing first base. The taunts and shouting of the fans were ringing in Pee Wee's ears. It saddened him, because he knew it could have been his friends and neighbors. Pee Wee's legs felt heavy, but he knew what he had to do.

As he walked toward Jackie wearing the gray Dodger uniform, he looked into his teammate's bold, pained eyes. The first baseman had done nothing to provoke the hostility except that he sought to be treated as an equal. Jackie was grim with anger. Pee Wee smiled broadly as he reached Jackie. Jackie smiled back.

Stopping beside Jackie, Pee Wee put his arm
around Jackie's shoulders. An audible gasp rose
up from the crowd when they saw what Pee Wee
had done. Then there was silence.

Outlined on a sea of green grass stood these
two great athletes, one black, one white, both
wearing the same team uniform.

"I am standing by him," Pee Wee Reese said to
the world. "This man is my teammate."

Concept Connections

Linking the Selection

Think about the following questions, and then record your responses in the Response Journal section of your Writer's Notebook.

- Jackie Robinson, the first African American player in the Major Leagues, was not always treated kindly. How did Pee Wee Reese show Jackie his friendship?

- Why was Pee Wee's friendship so important to Jackie?

Exploring Concept Vocabulary

The concept term for this lesson is **peer pressure.** If you do not know what this term means, look it up in a dictionary. Answer these questions:

- How can **peer pressure** endanger a friendship?

- How did Pee Wee Reese show his teammates and fans that he would not give in to **peer pressure?**

In the Vocabulary section of your Writer's Notebook, write a sentence using the term **peer pressure** and a word from the selection vocabulary.

Expanding the Concept

Think about the selections "Gloria Who Might Be My Best Friend," "Angel Child, Dragon Child," and "Teammates." What have these selections taught you about friendship?

Try to use the term *peer pressure* in your discussion about the selections and their characters.

Add new ideas about friendship to the Concept/Question Board.

Meet the Author

Peter Golenbock is a sportswriter who especially loves baseball. He remembers going to the World Series in 1956 with his uncle and afterward meeting Jackie Robinson. He says, *"I was 12 years old, and I'll never forget being struck by how large he was."* Throughout his career Peter Golenbock has had the opportunity to meet many famous players and to hear the stories they tell about the game's history. He has even written biographies about some of the players he has talked to. He is the author of many well-known books about sports, but this book was the first one he wrote for children.

Meet the Illustrator

Paul Bacon is an award-winning illustrator and famous designer of book jackets. He lives in Clintondale, New York, with his wife.

93

THE
LEGEND OF
DAMON AND PYTHIAS

adapted as a play by Fan Kissen
illustrated by Fabricio Vanden Broeck

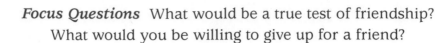

CAST

Damon	Second Robber
Pythias	First Voice
Soldier	Second Voice
King	Third Voice
Mother	Announcer
First Robber	Narrator

SOUNDS

Iron door open and shut   *Key in lock*

ANNOUNCER: Hello, listeners! It's story time again. Today's story is about the strong friendship between two men. Listen, and you'll hear how one of these men was ready to give up his life for his friend's sake.

MUSIC: (*Up full and out*)

NARRATOR: Long, long ago there lived on the island of Sicily two young men named Damon and Pythias. They were known far and wide for the strong friendship each had for the other. Their names have come down to our own times to mean true friendship. You may hear it said of two persons:

FIRST VOICE: Those two? Why, they're like Damon and Pythias!

NARRATOR: The King of that country was a cruel tyrant. He made cruel laws, and he showed no mercy toward anyone who broke his laws. Now, you might very well wonder:

SECOND VOICE: Why didn't the people rebel?

NARRATOR: Well, the people didn't dare rebel, because they feared the King's great and powerful army. No one dared say a word against the King or his laws—except Damon and Pythias. One day a soldier overheard Pythias speaking against a new law the King had proclaimed.

SOLDIER: Ho, there! Who are you, that dares to speak so about our King?

PYTHIAS: (*Unafraid*) I am called Pythias.

SOLDIER: Don't you know it is a crime to speak against the King or his laws? You are under arrest! Come and tell this opinion of yours to the King's face!

MUSIC: (*A few short bars in and out*)

NARRATOR: When Pythias was brought before the King, he showed no fear. He stood straight and quiet before the throne.

KING: (*Hard, cruel*) So, Pythias! They tell me you do not approve of the laws I make.

PYTHIAS: I am not alone, your Majesty, in thinking your laws are cruel. But you rule the people with such an iron hand that they dare not complain.

KING: (*Angry*) But *you* have the daring to complain *for* them! Have they appointed you their champion?

PYTHIAS: No, your Majesty. I speak for myself alone. I have no wish to make trouble for anyone. But I am not afraid to tell you that the people are suffering under your rule. They want to have a voice in making the laws for themselves. You do not allow them to speak up for themselves.

97

KING: In other words, you are calling me a tyrant! Well, you shall learn for yourself how a tyrant treats a rebel! Soldier! Throw this man into prison!

SOLDIER: At once, your Majesty! Don't try to resist, Pythias!

PYTHIAS: I know better than to try to resist a soldier of the King! And for how long am I to remain in prison, your Majesty, merely for speaking out for the people?

KING: (*Cruel*) Not for very long, Pythias. Two weeks from today at noon, you shall be put to death in the public square, as an example to anyone else who may dare to question my laws or acts. Off to prison with him, soldier!

MUSIC: (*In briefly and out*)

NARRATOR: When Damon heard that his friend Pythias had been thrown into prison, and the severe punishment that was to follow, he was heartbroken. He rushed to the prison and persuaded the guard to let him speak to his friend.

DAMON: Oh, Pythias! How terrible to find you here! I wish I could do something to save you!

PYTHIAS: Nothing can save me, Damon, my dear friend. I am prepared to die. But there is one thought that troubles me greatly.

DAMON: What is it? I will do anything to help you.

PYTHIAS: I'm worried about what will happen to my mother and my sister when I'm gone.

DAMON: I'll take care of them, Pythias, as if they were my own mother and sister.

PYTHIAS: Thank you, Damon. I have money to leave them. But there are other things I must arrange. If only I could go to see them before I die! But they live two days' journey from here, you know.

DAMON: I'll go to the King and beg him to give you your freedom for a few days. You'll give your word to return at the end of that time. Everyone in Sicily knows you for a man who has never broken his word.

PYTHIAS: Do you believe for one moment that the King would let me leave this prison, no matter how good my word may have been all my life?

DAMON: I'll tell him that *I* shall take your place in this prison cell. I'll tell him that if you do not return by the appointed day, he may kill *me*, in your place!

PYTHIAS: No, no, Damon! You must not do such a foolish thing! I cannot—I *will* not—let you do this! Damon! Damon! Don't go! (*To himself*) Damon, my friend! You may find yourself in a cell beside me!

MUSIC: (*In briefly and out*)

DAMON: (*Begging*) Your Majesty! I beg of you! Let Pythias go home for a few days to bid farewell to his mother and sister. He gives his word that he will return at your appointed time. Everyone knows that his word can be trusted.

KING: In ordinary business affairs—perhaps. But he is now a man under sentence of death. To free him even for a few days would strain his honesty—*any* man's honesty—too far. Pythias would never return here! I consider him a traitor, but I'm certain he's no fool.

DAMON: Your Majesty! I will take his place in the prison until he comes back. If he does not return, then you may take *my* life in his place.

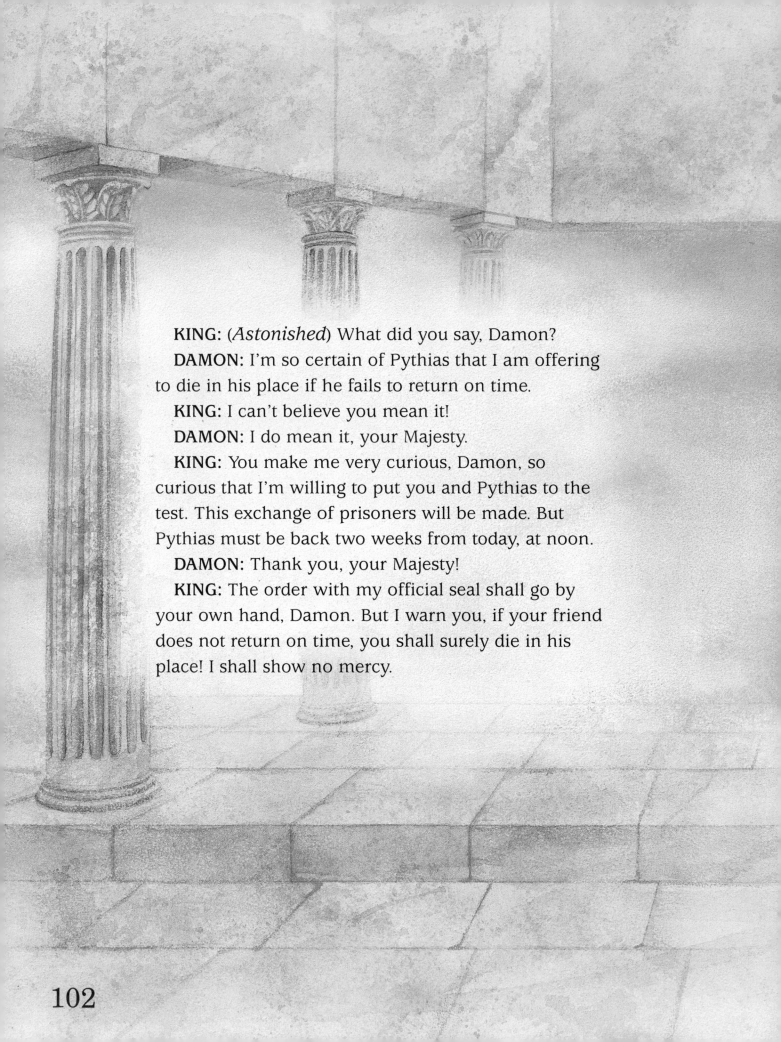

KING: (*Astonished*) What did you say, Damon?

DAMON: I'm so certain of Pythias that I am offering to die in his place if he fails to return on time.

KING: I can't believe you mean it!

DAMON: I do mean it, your Majesty.

KING: You make me very curious, Damon, so curious that I'm willing to put you and Pythias to the test. This exchange of prisoners will be made. But Pythias must be back two weeks from today, at noon.

DAMON: Thank you, your Majesty!

KING: The order with my official seal shall go by your own hand, Damon. But I warn you, if your friend does not return on time, you shall surely die in his place! I shall show no mercy.

MUSIC: (*In briefly and out*)

NARRATOR: Pythias did not like the King's bargain with Damon. He did not like to leave his friend in prison, with the chance that he might lose his life if something went wrong. But at last Damon persuaded him to leave, and Pythias set out for his home. More than a week went by. The day set for the death sentence drew near. Pythias did not return. Everyone in the city knew of the condition on which the King had permitted Pythias to go home. Everywhere people met, the talk was sure to turn to the two friends.

FIRST VOICE: Do you suppose Pythias will come back?

SECOND VOICE: Why should he stick his head under the King's axe, once he's escaped?

THIRD VOICE: Still, would an honorable man like Pythias let such a good friend die for him?

FIRST VOICE: There's no telling what a man will do when it's a question of his own life against another's.

SECOND VOICE: But if Pythias doesn't come back before the time is up, he will be killing his friend.

THIRD VOICE: Well, there's still a few days' time. I, for one, am certain that Pythias *will* return in time.

SECOND VOICE: And *I* am just as certain that he will *not*. Friendship is friendship, but a man's own life is something stronger, *I* say!

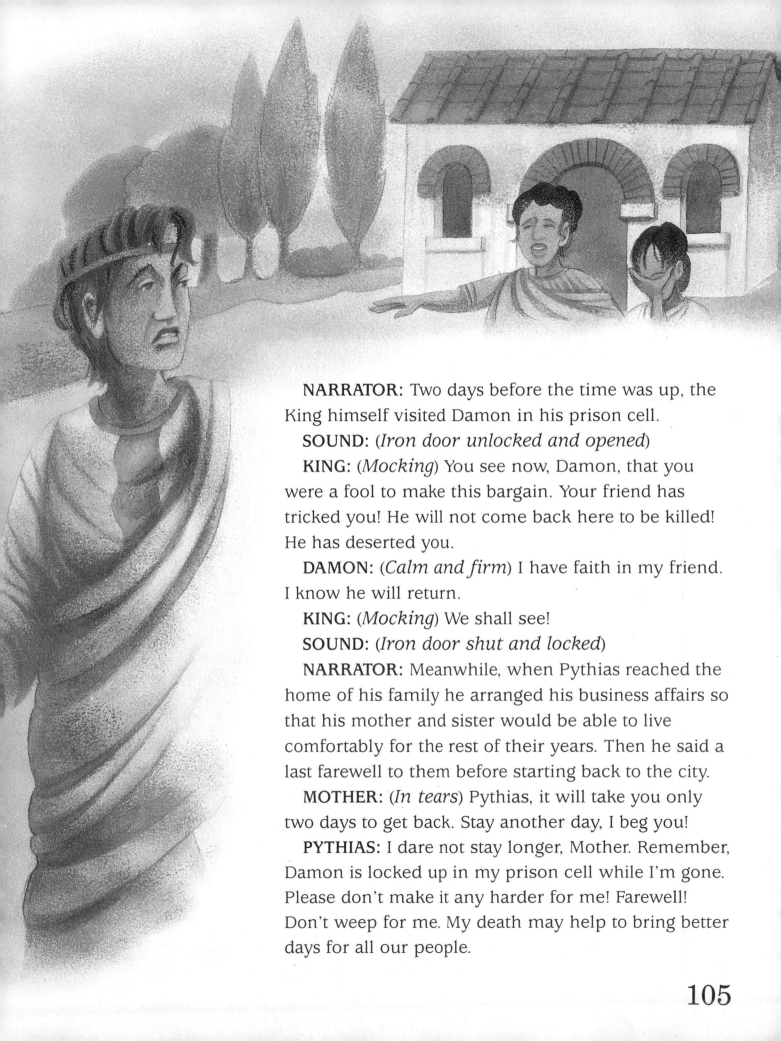

NARRATOR: Two days before the time was up, the King himself visited Damon in his prison cell.

SOUND: (*Iron door unlocked and opened*)

KING: (*Mocking*) You see now, Damon, that you were a fool to make this bargain. Your friend has tricked you! He will not come back here to be killed! He has deserted you.

DAMON: (*Calm and firm*) I have faith in my friend. I know he will return.

KING: (*Mocking*) We shall see!

SOUND: (*Iron door shut and locked*)

NARRATOR: Meanwhile, when Pythias reached the home of his family he arranged his business affairs so that his mother and sister would be able to live comfortably for the rest of their years. Then he said a last farewell to them before starting back to the city.

MOTHER: (*In tears*) Pythias, it will take you only two days to get back. Stay another day, I beg you!

PYTHIAS: I dare not stay longer, Mother. Remember, Damon is locked up in my prison cell while I'm gone. Please don't make it any harder for me! Farewell! Don't weep for me. My death may help to bring better days for all our people.

105

NARRATOR: So Pythias began his journey in plenty of time. But bad luck struck him on the very first day. At twilight, as he walked along a lonely stretch of woodland, a rough voice called:

FIRST ROBBER: Not so fast there, young man! Stop!

PYTHIAS: (*Startled*) Oh! What is it? What do you want?

SECOND ROBBER: Your money bags.

PYTHIAS: My money bags? I have only this small bag of coins. I shall need them for some favors, perhaps, before I die.

FIRST ROBBER: What do you mean, before you die? We don't mean to kill you, only take your money.

PYTHIAS: I'll give you my money, only don't delay me any longer. I am to die by the King's order three days from now. If I don't return to prison on time, my friend must die in my place.

FIRST ROBBER: A likely story! What man would be fool enough to go back to prison, ready to die.

SECOND ROBBER: And what man would be fool enough to die *for* you?

FIRST ROBBER: We'll take your money, all right. And we'll tie you up while we get away.

PYTHIAS: (*Begging*) No! No! I must get back to free my friend! (*Fade*) I must go back!

NARRATOR: But the two robbers took Pythias's money, tied him to a tree, and went off as fast as they could. Pythias struggled to free himself. He cried out for help as loud as he could, for a long time. But no one traveled through that lonesome woodland after dark. The sun had been up for many hours before he finally managed to free himself from the ropes that had tied him to the tree. He lay on the ground, hardly able to breathe.

MUSIC: (*In briefly and out*)

NARRATOR: After a while Pythias got to his feet. Weak and dizzy from hunger and thirst and his struggle to free himself, he set off again. Day and night he traveled without stopping, desperately trying to reach the city in time to save Damon's life.

MUSIC: (*Up and out*)

NARRATOR: On the last day, half an hour before noon, Damon's hands were tied behind his back and he was taken into the public square. The people muttered angrily as Damon was led in by the jailer. Then the King entered and seated himself on a high platform.

SOUND: (*Crowd voices in and hold under single voices*)

SOLDIER: (*Loud*) Long live the King!

FIRST VOICE: (*Low*) The longer he lives, the more miserable our lives will be!

KING: (*Loud, mocking*) Well, Damon, your lifetime is nearly up. Where is your good friend Pythias now?

DAMON: (*Firm*) I have faith in my friend. If he has not returned, I'm certain it is through no fault of his own.

KING: (*Mocking*) The sun is almost overhead. The shadow is almost at the noon mark. And still your friend has not returned to give you back your life!

DAMON: (*Quiet*) I am ready, and happy, to die in his place.

KING: (*Harsh*) And you shall, Damon! Jailer, lead the prisoner to the—

SOUND: (*Crowd voices up to a roar, then under*)

FIRST VOICE: (*Over noise*) Look! It's Pythias!

SECOND VOICE: (*Over noise*) Pythias has come back!

PYTHIAS: (*Breathless*) Let me through! Damon!

DAMON: Pythias!

PYTHIAS: Thank the gods I'm not too late!

DAMON: (*Quiet, sincere*) I would have died for you gladly, my friend.

CROWD VOICES: (*Loud, demanding*) Set them free! Set them both free!

KING: (*Loud*) People of the city! (*Crowd voices out*) Never in all my life have I seen such faith and friendship, such loyalty between men. There are many among you who call me harsh and cruel. But I cannot kill *any* man who proves such strong and true friendship for another. Damon and Pythias, I set you both free. (*Roar of approval from crowd*) I am King. I command a great army. I have stores of gold and precious jewels. But I would give all my money and power for one friend like Damon or Pythias.

SOUND: (*Roar of approval from crowd up briefly and out*)

MUSIC: (*Up and out*)

THE LEGEND OF DAMON AND PYTHIAS

Concept Connections

Linking the Selection

Think about the following questions, and then record your responses in the Response Journal section of your Writer's Notebook.

- What did Damon do to show his friendship for Pythias?

- How did the friendship of Damon and Pythias save their lives?

Exploring Concept Vocabulary

The concept word for this lesson is *sacrifice.* If you do not know what this word means, look it up in a dictionary. Answer these questions:

- What *sacrifice* did Damon make for Pythias? Why was Damon willing to make this *sacrifice?*

- What does Damon's *sacrifice* tell you about his friendship with Pythias?

In the Vocabulary section of your Writer's Notebook, write a sentence using the word *sacrifice* and one of the selection vocabulary words.

110

Expanding the Concept

Compare and contrast the friendships you have read about in this unit. How were the friendships alike and different? What conclusions can you draw about what makes a good friendship?

Try to use the word **sacrifice** in your discussion.

Add new ideas about friendship to the Concept/Question Board.

Meet the Author

Fan Kissen writes plays for eight to ten year olds. These plays often tell folktales and legends, such as the Greek myth of Damon and Pythias. She writes her plays in the same style as one would write a radio show, by including announcers, sound effects, and background music. She has received many awards for her successful radio series, *Tales from the Four Winds*. Kissen has traveled to South America, Europe, and the Near East. She speaks French, German, and a little Italian.

Meet the Illustrator

Fabricio Vanden Broeck was born in Mexico City. He went on to study art in Mexico and Europe. His illustrations have appeared in children's books, exhibits, and newspapers. Displays of Broeck's work have been shown around the world. In the United States, his illustrations have appeared in the famous newspaper, *The New York Times*.

City Wildlife

Even if you live in the city, wild things surround you. What are they? Where are they? How do they live? Maybe if you look, you will find them.

The Boy Who Didn't Believe in Spring

Lucille Clifton

illustrated by Brinton Turkle

Once upon a time there was a little boy named King Shabazz who didn't believe in Spring. "No such thing!" he would whisper every time the teacher talked about Spring in school.

"Where is it at?" he would holler every time his Mama talked about Spring at home.

114

He used to sit with his friend Tony Polito on the
bottom step when the days started getting longer and
warmer and talk about it.

"Everybody talkin bout Spring!" he would say to Tony.

"Big deal," Tony would say back.

"No such thing!" he would say to Tony.

"Right!" Tony would say back.

One day after the teacher had been talking about
birds that were blue and his Mama had started talking
about crops coming up, King Shabazz decided he had
just had enough. He put his jacket on and his shades
and went by for Tony Polito.

"Look here, man," King said when they got out to the
bottom step, "I'm goin to get me some of this Spring."

"What you mean, man?" Tony asked him.

"Everybody talkin bout Spring comin, and Spring just round the corner. I'm goin to go round there and see what do I see."

Tony Polito watched King Shabazz get up and push his shades up tight on his nose.

"You comin with me, man?" he said while he was pushing.

Tony Polito thought about it for a minute. Then he got up and turned his cap around backwards.

"Right!" Tony Polito said back.

King Shabazz and Tony Polito had been around the corner before, but only as far as the streetlight alone. They passed the school and the playground.

"Ain't no Spring in there," said King Shabazz with a laugh. "Sure ain't," agreed Tony Polito.

They passed Weissman's. They stopped for a minute by the side door at Weissman's and smelled the buns.

"Sure do smell good," whispered Tony.

"But it ain't Spring," King was quick to answer.

They passed the apartments and walked fast in case they met Junior Williams. He had said in school that he was going to beat them both up.

Then they were at the streetlight. Tony stopped and made believe his sneaker was untied to see what King was going to do. King stopped and blew on his shades to clean them and to see what Tony was going to do. They stood there for two light turns and then King Shabazz grinned at Tony Polito, and he grinned back, and the two boys ran across the street.

"Well, if we find it, it ought to be now," said King.

Tony didn't say anything. He just stood looking around.

"Well, come on, man," King whispered, and they started down the street.

They passed the Church of the Solid Rock with high windows all decorated and pretty.

They passed a restaurant with little round tables near the window. They came to a take-out shop and stood by the door a minute to smell the bar-b-q.

"Sure would like to have some of that," whispered King.

"Me too," whispered Tony with his eyes closed. They walked slower down the street.

Just after they passed some apartments King Shabazz and Tony Polito came to a vacant lot. It was small and had high walls from apartments on three sides of it. Three walls around it and right in the middle——a car!

It was beautiful. The wheels were gone and so were the doors, but it was dark red and sitting high on a dirt mound in the middle of the lot.

"Oh man, oh man," whispered King.

"Oh man," whispered Tony.

Then they heard the noise.

It was a little long sound, like smooth things rubbing against rough, and it was coming from the car. It happened again. King looked at Tony and grabbed his hand.

"Let's see what it is, man," he whispered. He thought Tony would say no and let's go home. Tony looked at King and held his hand tightly.

"Right," he said very slowly.

The boys stood there a minute, then began tiptoeing over toward the car. They walked very slowly across the lot. When they were halfway to the car, Tony tripped and almost fell. He looked down and saw a patch of little yellow pointy flowers, growing in the middle of short spiky green leaves.

"Man, I think you tripped on these crops!" King laughed.

"They're comin up," Tony shouted. "Man, the crops are comin up!"

And just as Tony was making all that noise, they
heard another noise, like a lot of things waving in the
air, and they looked over at the car and three birds flew
out of one of the door holes and up to the wall of the
apartment.

King and Tony ran over to the car to see where the
birds had been. They had to climb up a little to get to
the door and look in.

They stood there looking a long time without saying
anything. There on the front seat down in a whole lot
of cottony stuff was a nest. There in the nest were four
light blue eggs. Blue. King took off his shades.

"Man, it's Spring," he said almost to himself.

"Anthony Polito!"

King and Tony jumped down off the mound. Somebody was shouting for Tony as loud as he could.

"Anthony Polito!"

The boys turned and started walking out of the vacant lot. Tony's brother Sam was standing at the edge of the lot looking mad.

"Ma's gonna kill you, after I get finished, you squirt!" he hollered.

King Shabazz looked at Tony Polito and took his hand.

"Spring is here," he whispered to Tony.

"Right," whispered Tony Polito back.

The Boy Who Didn't Believe in Spring

Concept Connections

Linking the Selection

 Think about the following questions, and then record your responses in the Response Journal section of your Writer's Notebook.

- Why do you think King Shabazz did not believe in Spring?

- Where did the birds make their home in the vacant lot?

Exploring Concept Vocabulary

The concept word for this lesson is *wildlife.* If you do not know what this word means, look it up in a dictionary. Answer these questions:

- What kinds of *wildlife* did King and Tony see in the vacant lot?

- What other kinds of *wildlife* might King and Tony have seen in the vacant lot?

- What kinds of *wildlife* live near you?

Use the word *wildlife* and one of the selection vocabulary words in an oral sentence.

Expanding the Concept

Think about the Read Aloud "City Lots" and the story "The Boy Who Didn't Believe in Spring." What have you learned about city wildlife from these selections?

Try to use the word *wildlife* in your discussion.

Add new ideas about city wildlife to the Concept/Question Board.

Meet the Author

Lucille Clifton is a famous poet and writer of children's books. When she was just sixteen years old, she became the first member of her family to earn a scholarship and attend college. She knew while attending college that what she wanted most to be was a writer. However, it took her many years to reach her goal. Lucille Clifton first finished college, married, and had six children. When she did publish her first book, a book of poems called *Good Times*, *The New York Times* named it one of the ten best books of the year. Since then, she has won many awards and has become one of the most famous poets and children's authors.

Meet the Illustrator

Brinton Turkle is a famous illustrator of children's books as well as an author. He first studied drama for a while in college. Then he decided to focus more on drawing and went to school for fine arts.

He has written many famous children's books in the hope that they will teach children kindness, honesty, and a love for life.

City Critters:

Wild Animals Live in Cities, Too

by Richard Chevat

The city. Tall buildings. Shoppers with their arms full of packages. People hurrying along. Buses, cabs, cars—and wild animals.

Wild animals? You bet. Cities and towns are filled with wildlife.

"When most people think of wildlife, they think of grizzly bears or elk or white-tailed deer. But *all* the wild animals that live in a city are wildlife, including butterflies, ants, pigeons and even rats," says Mike Matthews. He's a scientist

These city ducks might cause a traffic jam.

126

who works for New York state, trying to protect its wildlife, both in the woods and in the cities.

Why does a rat deserve to be called "wildlife"? Charles Nilon, a biologist for the Kansas Department of Wildlife and Parks explains: "Any animal that you see that is not a pet, that doesn't depend on people taking care of it, is a wild animal."

Skyscraper Geese, Park Raccoons

On the tenth floor of an office building in St. Louis, Missouri, is a nest of Canadian geese. They've been spending summers there for the past six years.

Dave Tylka is an urban biologist—a scientist who studies wildlife in cities. He talked about the skyscraper geese. "There's a type of Canadian geese that nest on cliffs over the Mississippi River," he said. "These particular geese must have thought that a balcony looked like a good cliff to nest on!"

If geese on an office building sound strange, how about raccoons in the heart of New York City? Mike Matthews says they live in sewers, in buildings, and especially in New York's Central Park. "People think that animals want to be near trees or open spaces. But raccoons will live in chimneys and sewers."

Raccoons live in sewers and parks. They find food in garbage cans.

127

Bird's-Eye View

According to Matthews, city parks are great places to go bird-watching, especially in the early spring and fall. "They're like islands of green space where migrating birds will stop," he says.

When Mike Matthews talks about birds, he doesn't just mean "city birds" like sparrows, starlings and pigeons. "There's much, much more," he says. "In the city limits, there are great blue herons, owls and all sorts of water birds. Even a bald eagle will visit from time to time."

You might think these creatures would try to avoid cities. Not so, says Matthews. Animals will live wherever they can find food, shelter and a place to raise their young.

Scientists' Helpers

Scientists can learn a lot about a city by studying the wild animals that live there. "If you're concerned about pollution or waste, looking at wildlife is one way to learn about it," says Charles Nilon, the Kansas biologist.

"For example, in Florida, scientists studied squirrels that lived by highways. The scientists wanted to find out how the squirrels had been affected by breathing car exhaust. Because they breathe the fumes all day, any health problems will show up in squirrels before they

A street light makes a good perch for this eagle.

128

Squirrels and chipmunks are common wildlife in cities.
This chipmunk is stealing some birdseed from a window ledge.

show up in humans."

Sometimes, very rare animals can survive well in cities. Take the peregrine falcon. This bird had almost disappeared in the eastern United States. About 15 years ago, scientists began trying to save the peregrine falcon by raising baby falcons in laboratories and releasing them in the wild.

Today, the bird is making a comeback, and several falcons have come back to nest in the middle of big cities. There, they've found just the right kinds of shelter and food. They rest on skyscraper "cliffs," and they hunt city birds—pigeons and starlings.

Home Sweet City Home

Not all animals find city homes as easily as falcons have. That's why scientists create and protect special animal habitats—spots with the right amounts of water and food and the kinds of trees and plants an animal needs to survive.

At the Gateway National Recreation Area in New York City, scientists have set aside a small "grasslands" habitat—a flat, open field. Don Reipe, a scientist at Gateway, explained why: "Grasslands are vanishing because they're used for homes, shopping malls and other developments. But it's an important habitat for animals like the upland sandpiper, the meadowlark and the short-eared owl. Our grasslands area is a home to all these birds."

Scientists in Des Moines, Iowa, built a different kind of habitat—a garden that grows goodies for butterflies. It's in the state fairgrounds. "We planted a garden designed to attract 40 different species of butterflies," says Laura Jackson, an Iowa biologist. "The idea is to show people how they can attract butterflies to their backyards by planting the right flowers and plants."

Deer are moving closer to cities. Some have been spotted in city parks.

Do It Yourself

Most people don't see the wild animals all around them—because they don't know what to look for. Stephen Petland, a biologist in Seattle, Washington, says careful observation—and a look at a few bird and animal guides—can make the difference.

"In one neighborhood in Seattle, over the course of a year, I might be able to find 40 or 50 different types of birds," notes Petland.

You don't have to be a scientist to study wildlife in cities or towns. Just keep an eagle eye when you're playing in your yard, your playground or your neighborhood park. And when you're walking down the street, don't forget: Watch out for wild animals!

131

City Critters:

Wild Animals Live in Cities, Too

Concept Connections

Linking the Selection

Think about the following questions, and then record your responses in the Response Journal section of your Writer's Notebook.

- Where are some of the places that wild animals live in the city?

- What do wild animals need to survive in the city?

Exploring Concept Vocabulary

The concept word for this lesson is **adapt.** If you do not know what this word means, look it up in a dictionary. Answer these questions:

- How do wild animals **adapt** to living in the city?

- Why is it important for wildlife to **adapt** to its surroundings?

Think about the word **adapt** and the selection vocabulary words. Then make up an oral sentence using the concept word and one of the selection vocabulary words.

Expanding the Concept

Think about the selection "City Critters" and the story "The Boy Who Didn't Believe in Spring." Where else could King and Tony have looked for spring in the city?

Try to include the word **adapt** in your discussion.

Add new ideas about city wildlife to the Concept/Question Board.

Meet the Author

Richard Chevat loved to read and make up stories of his own as a child in New York City. Today he lives in New Jersey with his wife, two children, and a pet bird named Madonna. He writes at home while his children are at school and his wife is at work. *"I play the guitar, I like to cook, and spend a lot of time with my kids,"* says Mr. Chevat.

Focus Questions What are some characteristics of raccoons? How can raccoons be referred to as both annoying and admirable?

Raccoon

Mary Ann Hoberman
illustrated by Pamela Carroll

Crash goes the trashcan! Clatter and clacket!
What in the world can be making that racket?
I hurry to look by the light of the moon.
And what do I find? Why, a fine fat raccoon!
All through the garden the garbage he's strewn,
And he's eating his supper, that robber raccoon,
Eating so nicely without fork or spoon,
Why, his manners are perfect, that thieving raccoon!
And wasn't he smart to discover that pail?
And wasn't he smart to uncover that pail?
And isn't he lucky he won't go to jail
For stealing his dinner and making a mess
For me to clean up in the morning, I guess,
While he, the old pirate, abundantly fed,
Curls up in a ball fast asleep in his bed.

Focus Questions How can an environment be both safe and dangerous for its wildlife? How do various types of city wildlife adapt to their environments? What role do people play in protecting the natural environment?

Make Way For Ducklings

by Robert McCloskey

M r. and Mrs. Mallard were looking for a place to live. But every time Mr. Mallard saw what looked like a nice place, Mrs. Mallard said it was no good. There were sure to be foxes in the woods or turtles in the water, and she was not going to raise a family where there might be foxes or turtles. So they flew on and on.

When they got to Boston, they felt too tired to fly any further. There was a nice pond in the Public Garden, with a little island on it. "The very place to spend the night," quacked Mr. Mallard. So down they flapped.

Next morning they fished for their breakfast in the mud at the bottom of the pond. But they didn't find much.

136

Just as they were getting ready to start on their way, a strange enormous bird came by. It was pushing a boat full of people, and there was a man sitting on its back. "Good morning," quacked Mr. Mallard, being polite. The big bird was too proud to answer. But the people on the boat threw peanuts into the water, so the Mallards followed them all round the pond and got another breakfast, better than the first.

"I like this place," said Mrs. Mallard as they climbed out on the bank and waddled along. "Why don't we build a nest and raise our ducklings right in this pond? There are no foxes and no turtles, and the people feed us peanuts. What could be better?"

"Good," said Mr. Mallard, delighted that at last Mrs. Mallard had found a place that suited her. But——

137

"Look out!" squawked Mrs. Mallard, all of a dither. "You'll get run over!" And when she got her breath she added: "*This* is no place for babies, with all those horrid things rushing about. We'll have to look somewhere else."

So they flew over Beacon Hill and round the State House, but there was no place there.

They looked in Louisburg Square, but there was no water to swim in.

Then they flew over the Charles River. "This is better," quacked Mr. Mallard. "That island looks like a nice quiet place, and it's only a little way from the Public Garden." "Yes," said Mrs. Mallard, remembering the peanuts. "That looks like just the right place to hatch ducklings."

So they chose a cozy spot among the bushes near the water and settled down to build their nest. And only just in time, for now they were beginning to molt. All their old wing feathers started to drop out, and they would not be able to fly again until the new ones grew in.

But of course they could swim, and one day they swam over to the park on the river bank, and there they met a policeman called Michael. Michael fed them peanuts, and after that the Mallards called on Michael every day.

After Mrs. Mallard had laid eight eggs in the nest she couldn't go to visit Michael any more, because she had to sit on the eggs to keep them warm. She moved off the nest only to get a drink of water, or to have her lunch, or to count the eggs and make sure they were all there.

One day the ducklings hatched out. First came Jack, then Kack, and then Lack, then Mack and Nack and Ouack and Pack and Quack. Mr. and Mrs. Mallard were bursting with pride. It was a great

responsibility taking care of so many ducklings, and it kept them very busy.

One day Mr. Mallard decided he'd like to take a trip to see what the rest of the river was like, further on. So off he set. "I'll meet you in a week, in the Public Garden," he quacked over his shoulder. "Take good care of the ducklings."

"Don't you worry," said Mrs. Mallard. "I know all about bringing up children." And she did.

She taught them how to swim and dive.

She taught them to walk in a line, to come when they were called, and to keep a safe distance from bikes and scooters and other things with wheels.

When at last she felt perfectly satisfied with them, she said one morning: "Come along, children. Follow me." Before you could wink an eyelash Jack, Kack, Lack, Mack, Nack, Ouack, Pack, and Quack fell into line, just as they had been taught. Mrs. Mallard led the way into the water and they swam behind her to the opposite bank.

There they waded ashore and waddled along till they came to the highway.

Mrs. Mallard stepped out to cross the road. "Honk, honk!" went the horns on the speeding cars. "Qua-a-ack!" went Mrs. Mallard as she tumbled back again. "Quack! Quack! Quack! Quack!" went Jack, Kack, Lack, Mack, Nack, Ouack, Pack, and Quack, just as loud as their little quackers could quack. The cars kept speeding by and honking, and Mrs. Mallard and the ducklings kept right on quack-quack-quacking.

They made such a noise that Michael came running, waving his arms and blowing his whistle.

He planted himself in the center of the road, raised one hand to stop the traffic, and then beckoned with the other, the way policemen do, for Mrs. Mallard to cross over.

As soon as Mrs. Mallard and the ducklings were safe on the other side and on their way down Mount Vernon Street, Michael rushed back to his police booth.

He called Clancy at headquarters and said: "There's a family of ducks walkin' down the street!" Clancy said: "Family of *what?*" "*Ducks!*" yelled Michael. "Send a police car, quick!"

Meanwhile Mrs. Mallard had reached the Corner Book Shop and turned into Charles Street, with Jack, Kack, Lack, Mack, Nack, Ouack, Pack, and Quack all marching in line behind her.

Everyone stared. An old lady from Beacon Hill said: "Isn't it

amazing!" and the man who swept the streets said: "Well, now, ain't that nice!" and when Mrs. Mallard heard them she was so proud she tipped her nose in the air and walked along with an extra swing in her waddle.

When they came to the corner of Beacon Street there was the police car with four policemen that Clancy had sent from headquarters. The policemen held back the traffic so Mrs. Mallard and the ducklings could march across the street, right on into the Public Garden.

Inside the gate they all turned round to say thank you to the policemen. The policemen smiled and waved good-by.

When they reached the pond and swam across to the little island, there was Mr. Mallard waiting for them, just as he had promised.

The ducklings liked the new island so much that they decided to live there. All day long they follow the swan boats and eat peanuts.

And when night falls they swim to their little island and go to sleep.

Make Way for Ducklings

Concept Connections
Linking the Selection

Think about the following questions, and then record your responses in the Response Journal section of your Writer's Notebook.

- What was important to Mr. and Mrs. Mallard as they looked for a good home in the city?

- How did the people in the story help protect Mr. and Mrs. Mallard and their family?

Exploring Concept Vocabulary

The concept word for this lesson is **environment.** If you do not know what this word means, look it up in a dictionary. Answer these questions:

- Describe the **environment** of Mr. and Mrs. Mallard's new home.

- What other kinds of wildlife might also be living in this **environment?**

In the Vocabulary section of your Writer's Notebook, write a sentence using the word **environment** and a selection vocabulary word.

Expanding the Concept

Think about the Mallards in "Make Way for Ducklings."
How are these fictional characters like the city wildlife in
"City Critters"? Try to use the word *environment* in your
discussion of city wildlife. Add new ideas about city wildlife
to the Concept/Question Board.

Meet the Author and Illustrator

Robert McCloskey learned to play the piano
and the harmonica as a boy. He also learned about
small engines and inventions. He even thought for a
while that he wanted to be an inventor. Then he
began drawing and became very good at it. After
high school, Robert McCloskey went on to study
art in Boston, New York, and Rome, Italy. To
prepare for writing *Make Way for Ducklings*,
Robert McCloskey bought four mallard ducks
to observe and sketch. It took him two years
to plan what he wanted to write about and
another two to write and draw it. His hard
work and patience paid off. He won a Caldecott
Medal, an important award for children's books,
for *Make Way for Ducklings*. The story is now
considered a classic. Robert McCloskey went on to
win a second Caldecott Medal, a very rare honor, for
his book *Time of Wonder*.

Lunch in the Gardens. 1985. **Beryl Cook.** Oil on masonite.
From Beryl Cook's New York, John Murray Publishing.

Cable Car Festival. 1988. **Dong Kingman.** Watercolor on paper. 30" × 22". Conacher Gallery, San Francisco.

147

Urban Roosts
Where Birds Nest in the City

from the book by
Barbara Bash

Early in the morning you can hear something rustling up on the ledge of an old stone building. Even before the city awakens, the birds are stirring in their urban roosts.

All across the country, as their natural habitats have been destroyed, birds have moved to town. The ones that have been able to adapt are thriving in the heart of the city.

One familiar urban dweller is the pigeon. Long ago it was called a rock dove, because it lived in the rocky cliffs along the coast of Europe. Today it flourishes all over the United States in the nooks and crannies of our cities.

148

To the pigeon, the city may look like a wilderness full of high cliffs and deep canyons. The cliffs are buildings made of stone and brick and glass, and the canyons are windy avenues full of cars and people. Flying together in flocks, pigeons explore the city canyons looking for food and spots to roost.

A roost is a place where birds go for protection when they sleep and for shelter from the rain and cold. Pigeons roost under highway overpasses, on window ledges, under building archways, on top of roofs, and under eaves. Sometimes their roosts are so well hidden you have to watch carefully to find them.

Look up under the train trestle. Pigeons may be roosting along the dark beams. Watch the open windows of an abandoned building. Hundreds of pigeons could be living inside, flying in and out all day long.

A nest is a place where birds lay their eggs and raise their chicks. Often it's in the same spot as the roost. Pigeons build a flimsy platform of sticks and twigs and debris up on a ledge, or on a windowsill, or in a flowerpot out on a fire escape, or in the curve of a storefront letter.

Throughout the year, pigeons lay eggs and hatch their young. The female sits quietly on her clutch, and after eighteen days, fuzzy chicks begin to appear. Five weeks later, after their adult feathers are fully developed, the young pigeons fly away to find homes of their own.

150

Sparrows and finches are successful city dwellers, too. Introduced from England in 1870 to control insects, the house sparrow has chosen to live close to people all across the United States. The house finch was originally a West Coast native, but some caged birds were released on the East Coast in 1940, and the species quickly spread. Sparrows and finches don't migrate, so you can watch them at backyard feeders throughout the year, chirping and chattering as they pick up seeds.

HOUSE SPARROW
female

male

male

female
HOUSE FINCH

The little hollows in and around building ornaments and Gothic sculptures are favorite nesting spots for sparrows and finches. These cavity nesters can slip into the tiniest spaces. Some of their nests are visible and others are completely hidden from view.

In the spring, you may see a small bird flying overhead with a twig in its beak. If you follow its flight, it will lead you to its nest.

Watch the bird land and then disappear into a crevice or behind a stone curve. A few moments later it will pop out again, empty-beaked, and fly away to search for more nesting material.

Sparrows and finches can even find spots to nest out in the middle of the busiest intersections. At the top of some streetlights, there's a small opening where the lamp meets the pole. If you look carefully, you may see a tiny house finch slip inside.

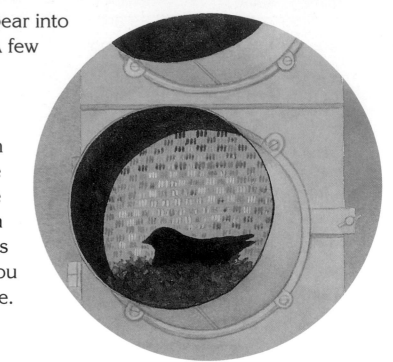

Or watch the short open pipe at the top of some traffic light poles. A pair of house sparrows may be darting in and out, bringing food to their nestlings. Sometimes you can even spot a nest in the metal casing that surrounds a traffic light. Perhaps the heat of the bulb keeps the eggs warm.

A tiled roof can house so many sparrows and finches it looks a little like an apartment complex. All day long the birds bring nesting material and food for their chicks into the small hidden cavities behind the tiles. When the chicks get too big for the nest, they play on top of the tiles, testing their wings before their first flight.

Because the house wren eats only insects, it prefers to live in the suburbs, where there are more bugs. The wren's family name is *Troglodytidae*, which means "creeper into holes." True to its name, the house wren can be found in the most unusual cavities: a work glove hanging on a line, a ball of twine, a teapot, an old shoe. Once the female wren chooses the cavity, she bolsters it with lots of nesting material to protect her eggs from intruders.

Along with the usual grasses, twigs, and feathers, wrens' nests have been found to contain hairpins, Kleenex, nails, wire, shoe buckles, candy wrappers, Band-Aids, paper clips, even dollar bills!

The barn owl lives in the city, too, but few people see it because it flies while everyone sleeps. All night long its pale, ghostly form soars over the buildings as it hunts for rats and mice to bring to its young.

The barn owl's eyes can see in the dark and its ears can hear the tiniest scratching. Even its voice is suited to city life; when it cries out in the night, it sounds like brakes screeching.

At daybreak, barn owls return to their nests to sleep. They like to live under train and highway overpasses and inside old barns and steeples. Instead of building nests, they lay their eggs in flat, protected spots. As baby barn owls grow, they huddle together, hissing and slurping, as they wait for their parents to return with food.

The nighthawk is a ground-nesting bird; it looks for a level, open surface on which to lay its eggs. Because city ground is full of cars and people, the nighthawk often hatches its young up on flat graveled rooftops.

If you look up on a warm summer night, you might see a nighthawk swooping low over the streetlights sweeping hundreds of insects into its large, gaping mouth. Or you might hear its call in the dark . . . *peent* . . . *peent* . . . .

Like the nighthawk, the killdeer makes no nest. It lays its eggs out in the open, in spots where the mottled eggshell pattern will be well camouflaged. In the city you might find killdeer eggs sitting on the gravel at the edge of a parking lot or next to a train track. Once, killdeer eggs were even found along the end line of a soccer field!

During the winter, crows flock together in large groups. They roost at night in the

tops of trees in city parks. At dusk, one or two arrive first, perching on high branches and making a silky rustle with their wings. As the light fades, more crows appear and the clamor increases. They make rattling sounds, catlike cries, and metallic squeaks while they jostle for spots. As the darkness deepens, the calls gradually die down, until only an occasional gurgle is heard. Then the crows settle in for the night.

In November, snowy owls migrate down from the arctic tundra to spend the winter in northern cities. They seem to like the windswept environment of airport landing fields—perhaps because it reminds them of home. The owls roost out on the open ground, blending in with the snowy whiteness.

At dusk the snowy owls begin hunting for mice, rats, and rabbits. They fly slowly and silently, their heads turning from side to side, their eyes scanning the ground for movement. Sometimes snowy owls will crouch on a small mound of snow and wait, completely still, for prey to wander by. The sound of the jets doesn't seem to faze them at all.

Cars and trucks lumber noisily over big city bridges. But underneath, hidden among the beams and girders, peregrine falcons have found a home. Sleekly built with powerful wings, the falcon is one of the fastest birds on earth. In the city it soars high above the bridges and buildings, hunting for pigeons and small birds flying below. When it spots its prey, the falcon folds its wings tight against its body and dives straight down at speeds of over one hundred fifty miles per hour!

In cities all across the country, people are fascinated with the peregrine falcon and are doing what they can to make this noble bird feel welcome. In many cities people set nesting boxes filled with gravel out on skyscraper ledges. The falcons seem to like these windy, rocky heights, for they return to the boxes early each spring to lay their eggs and raise their chicks. Living on these high perches with no natural enemies and plenty of pigeons, the falcons are adapting well to urban life.

So many birds make their homes in the midst of the city—sparrows and finches, barn owls and snowy owls, nighthawks and killdeers, pigeons and wrens, crows, and falcons. Each has found its own urban roost.

Urban Roosts
Where Birds Nest in the City

Concept Connections
Linking the Selection

Think about the following questions, and then record your responses in the Response Journal section of your Writer's Notebook.

- How are the birds' homes in the city like the homes they would have away from the city?

- Why are these similarities important?

Exploring Concept Vocabulary

The concept word for this lesson is **shelter.** If you do not know what this word means, look it up in a dictionary. Answer these questions:

- Why is it important for city wildlife to have **shelter?**

- What kinds of **shelter** did the birds find in the city?

In the Vocabulary section of your Writer's Notebook, write a sentence that includes the word **shelter** and one of the selection vocabulary words.

Expanding the Concept

Think about the city wildlife in the selection "City Critters." How are the birds in "Urban Roosts" similar to other city wildlife?

Try to use the word **shelter** in your discussion about the similarities.

Add new ideas about city wildlife to the Concept/Question Board.

Meet the Author and Illustrator

Barbara Bash began her love of art through her love of letters. *"My first connection to art and creativity was through the alphabet. I loved to draw the twenty-six letters. All through elementary school I experimented with their forms constantly."* Her love for art and letters led her to study calligraphy, the art of making fancy letters. From there, she went on to study nature and began learning how to draw it. Her love of nature gave her the desire to create books for children.

Before she writes a book, she learns everything she can about the subject through books, photographs, and films. Then she travels to the area where she can watch the subject. She has gone to Arizona to learn about the cactus and to East Africa to learn about the baobab tree. For this book, Barbara Bash walked through New York City to find where birds make their nests in the city.

163

Focus Questions What do you know about worms? Where are you most likely to find a worm? In what ways are worms fascinating?

The Worm

Raymond Souster
illustrated by Robert Byrd

Don't ask me how he managed
to corkscrew his way
through the King Street Pavement,
I'll leave that to you.

All I know is
there he was,
circling, uncoiling
his shining three inches,
wiggling all ten toes
as the warm rain fell
in that dark morning street
of early April.

Pigeons

Lilian Moore
illustrated by Robert Byrd

Pigeons are city folk
content
to live with concrete
and cement.

They seldom
try
the sky.

A pigeon never sings
of hill
and flowering hedge,
but busily commutes
from sidewalk
to his ledge.

Oh pigeon, what a waste of wings!

Focus Questions How do you think deer find their way into the city? What can be done to protect the deer in the city?

Two Days in May

Harriet Peck Taylor
illustrated by Leyla Torres

Early one Saturday morning in May, I went to our fire escape window and rubbed the sleep from my eyes. I looked down at the small garden I had planted behind our apartment building. Five animals were grazing on the new lettuce in my garden!

"Mama! Mama!" I called. "Come see what's in our yard!"

Mama hurried over to the window and gasped. "Sonia, those animals are deer, but how did they get here?" she asked. "I'll run and tell Mr. Donovan."

By the time Papa and I got out to the courtyard, a small crowd was gathering.

"Papa, why are there deer in the city?" I asked.

"The deer may have come all this way looking for food. They probably smelled your garden," he explained.

I thought I had never seen such an amazing sight. Their fur was a golden brown, and they balanced on tiny hooves. They had nervous tails, and eyes that were big and black and gentle.

Down the block a train rumbled by, but here life seemed to stand still. Pigeons and squirrels were almost the only birds or animals we ever saw in our neighborhood.

Looking around, I recognized many neighbors. There was Isidro Sánchez and his sister, Ana. Standing near me were Mr. Smiley, owner of Smiley's Laundromat, and my best friend, Peach, and Chester and Clarence Martin and the Yasamura sisters from down the hall. I saw Mr. Benny, the taxi driver, and the old Pigeon Lady, who was smiling brightly. I noticed that even neighbors who were almost strangers were standing close to each other and whispering in a friendly way. Well, everyone except Mr. Smiley and the Pigeon Lady, who were not on speaking terms. Mr. Smiley was angry because the Pigeon Lady fed her pigeons in front of his Laundromat, and he thought that was bad for business.

Mr. Donovan, our landlord, approached Papa. They spoke in hushed voices, but I was all ears.

"Luis, I, too, think the deer are really beautiful, but we both know they can't stay here," whispered Mr. Donovan. "They could be hit by a car. They belong in the woods, not in the city. I think we'd better call the animal control officers."

Papa nodded solemnly, and they walked off.

The Pigeon Lady came up to Peach and me and said, "Oh, girls, aren't they wonderful!"

"Yes!" we both answered together.

"I think two of the deer may be smaller. Those are probably females, or does. The males are called bucks. I used to see deer many years ago when I lived in the country."

Soon, Papa and Mr. Donovan returned with worried looks on their faces. They gathered the group together.

"The animal control office wants to shoot the deer," said Papa. "It's the law. The city is afraid the deer will starve."

"There aren't enough woods left for all the deer to find a home," added Mr. Donovan. "That's why the young deer wander far away. They're looking for territory of their own."

Everyone was so quiet that all you could hear was street sounds: honking and beeping, rumbling and humming.

Mr. Benny was the first to speak. "We can't let them shoot the deer. There must be another way."

"Yeah! That's right!" said Teresa Yasamura.

All around, people were nodding in agreement.

Then Chester spoke up. "They wouldn't shoot the deer in front of this many people. It would be too dangerous."

"It's true!" exclaimed Papa. "We can form a human wall around the deer without getting too close."

"Right on!" said Isidro. "We'll stay here until we can figure out what to do."

And that was the beginning of our peaceful protest.

Mr. Benny wrinkled his brow. "I remember reading a few months back about an organization that rescues and relocates animals that are stranded or injured. A fox had been hit by a car but wasn't badly hurt. This outfit took it in until it healed and then found a new home for it far from busy streets. I'll go see if I can find the number."

A little while later, Mr. Benny returned and announced, "The wildlife rescuer isn't in at the moment, but I left a message for him to call. I said it was an emergency."

When the animal control officer arrived, he saw the crowd surrounding the deer and decided not to take any chances. "If you don't mind, folks," he said, "I'll just hang around until you've all had enough and gone home." But we weren't leaving.

We stayed all afternoon, waiting anxiously, hoping to hear from the rescue organization. We got to know one another better, and we learned more about the deer.

Peach's eyes were wide and bright. "Look how they rotate their big soft ears to the left and right," she exclaimed.

Clarence said, "We studied deer in science. Their hearing is very sharp. It helps them detect enemies approaching from far away."

Mr. Benny nodded as he walked over to us. "I sometimes see this kind of deer at night, in the headlights, when I drive way past the city limits. When they're startled by the taxi's lights, their tails go up like flags. The tails are white underneath, which means the animals are white-tailed deer."

The deer grazed and slept cautiously, always alert to danger. They watched us with curious, intelligent eyes. I could see that the people made them uncomfortable, and it helped me appreciate that these really were wild animals. We tried to keep our distance and not make any sudden movements.

When evening came, the crowd grew. We talked quietly and told jokes as we kept watch over our silent friends. We ordered pizza from Giuseppe's.

Ana Sánchez spoke to the animal control officer. "Would you like a slice of pizza?" she asked.

"Thanks so much," he said. "My name is Steve Scully, and I understand how hard this must be for all of you. This is the part of my job I dislike.

"The problem is population growth. We've built towns and highways where there were once forests and streams. Now there is very little habitat left for the deer. There is no easy solution." He shook his head sadly.

I begged Papa to let me sleep outside all night, since almost everyone was staying. Mama came out with my baby brother, Danny. She brought blankets, a quilt, a jacket, and even my stuffed dog, Hershey.

Mama sat close and draped her arm across my shoulders. "Are you sure you'll be warm enough, Sonia?" she asked.

"I'm sure," I said.

We sat silently together, admiring the deer.

Finally she said, "I have to go put Danny to bed." She kissed me on the top of my head. "Sweet dreams, pumpkin."

I slept like a bear cub, curled in a ball against Papa's broad back.

Next morning, I awoke with the sun in my eyes and city sounds buzzing in my ears. Papa hugged me and asked how I liked camping out.

"I dreamed I was sleeping with the deer in cool forests under tall trees."

"You were, Sonia!" he said, laughing. "But not in the forest."

I looked at the deer. "Has the wildlife rescuer called back?" I asked.

"Yes, Sonia. The organization called late last night and hopes to get someone out here this morning."

The group was quiet as we all continued to wait.

Later that morning, a rusty orange truck pulled up. The man who got out had a friendly, open face. All eyes were on him.

"Hi, folks. My name is Carl Jackson, and I'm with the wildlife rescue organization," he said. "I need to put the deer in crates in order to take them to our center. Don't be alarmed—I'm going to shoot them with a small amount of tranquilizer to make them sleep for a little while." Then, as they wobbled on unsteady legs, he grabbed them gently and guided them toward the wooden crates.

Carl turned to the crowd and smiled. "I'm an animal lover, too, and all of you should feel proud for helping save these deer. I'll find a home for them in the woods, where they'll be safe and happy and have plenty to eat."

Steve Scully came forward and extended his hand to Carl. "Glad you came, man."

A cheer went up from the crowd. People slapped each other on the back. Isidro high-fived everyone, including Mr. Donovan and the Pigeon Lady. Peach and I hugged each other, and Papa shook hands with Carl and Steve. I said goodbye to Teresa and Sandy Yasamura and to Mr. Benny.

I even saw Mr. Smiley shake the Pigeon Lady's hand. "Maybe you can feed the pigeons *behind* my Laundromat," he said. "I have a little space back there."

The Pigeon Lady smiled.

A few days later, Papa got a call from Carl. One of the does had given birth to two fawns! And Carl had found a home for all seven deer in a wooded area northwest of the city.

Sometimes, when I'm sitting on the fire escape, watching the flickering city lights, I think of the deer. In my mind, they're gliding silently across tall grass meadows all aglow in silver moonlight.

Two Days in May

Concept Connections
Linking the Selection

Think about the following questions, and then record your responses in the Response Journal section of your Writer's Notebook.

- Why would Sonia's garden in the city not make a good home for the deer?
- "Two Days in May" is based on a true story. Why are more and more deer coming to the cities?

Exploring Concept Vocabulary

The concept word for this lesson is **protect.** If you do not know what this word means, look it up in a dictionary. Answer these questions:

- How does wildlife **protect** itself from things in the city that might harm it?
- How did the people in Sonia's neighborhood **protect** the deer?

In the Vocabulary section of your Writer's Notebook, write a sentence using the word **protect** and one of the selection vocabulary words.

Expanding the Concept

Think about the selections you have read in this unit. How is the wildlife in "Two Days in May" similar to the wildlife in "Make Way for Ducklings"? How is it different from the wildlife in "City Critters" and "Urban Roosts"?

Try to use the word **protect** in your discussion.

Add new ideas about city wildlife to the Concept/Question Board.

Meet the Author

Harriet Peck Taylor grew up in a family who painted, told stories, and camped. All these activities inspired her to become an artist. In elementary school, she wrote and illustrated picture books. She shows these books as she makes presentations to schools across the country, even though they get a few laughs for their simple drawings. Because Taylor has had pets throughout her life, animals have been one of her favorite things to write about. To young, aspiring writers she advises, *"Write about what you care about and what really excites you. In that way, you will be inspired to write it and it will be fun for you."*

Meet the Illustrator

Leyla Torres was raised in Bogotá, Colombia. In Colombia, her parents ran an elementary school. It was there that Torres began to enjoy reading and art. It had been her dream to visit New York City to see all of the art museums. Her aunt and uncle offered her a place to stay for a year in the city. Her experience at the New York Public Library inspired Torres's writing and illustrations. She says, *"I had never seen so many children's books in one place. The desire to do my own book blossomed and each author was like a teacher to me."*

Focus Questions What would it be like to discover a secret place in the city that animals call home? Why is it so important to protect such a secret place? What can you do to help protect the wildlife near you?

Secret Place

Eve Bunting
illustrated by Ted Rand

In the heart of the city where I live
there is a secret place.
Close by is a freeway
where cars and trucks boom,
and a railroad track
with freight trains that shunt and grunt.

There are warehouses
with windows blinded by dust
and names paint-scrawled on their brick walls.

The lines on the telephone and electric poles
web the sky.
Smokestacks blow clouds to dim the sun.

But in the heart of the city where I live,
low down, hidden,
a river runs.
The water is dark and shallow
in its concrete bed.
Bushes and tangled weeds
cling to the slopes of the concrete walls.

Hardly anyone knows the river is here.
Hardly anyone cares.

Mrs. Arren knows,
and Mr. Ramirez,
and Peter and Janet who are married.

I know, and my father knows, too.
He works a forklift
in one of the brick warehouses,
and I showed him the secret place
the day I found it.

The white egret found it, too.
I watch the bird float down,
its legs thin and reaching,
its head plumes fanned.

The green-winged teal knows.
The buffleheads that come to water-skim know.
And the circling mallards know.
I've seen them here before.
Peter says last year
there was a mallard nest
lined with feathers from the mother's breast.
Later there were ducklings.
"They'll nest here again," Peter says.
I jump up and down. "Ducklings! Perfect!"

sparrows

mallard.

Mrs. Arren and Mr. Ramirez and Janet and Peter
bring binoculars.
They let me look through them.
The sparrows lined up on the barbed wire fence
seem big as mud hens.

Peter tells me the names of the birds.
He is like a bird himself,
with hair the color of a cinnamon teal.

bufflehead.

coot

cinnamon teal

green-winged teal

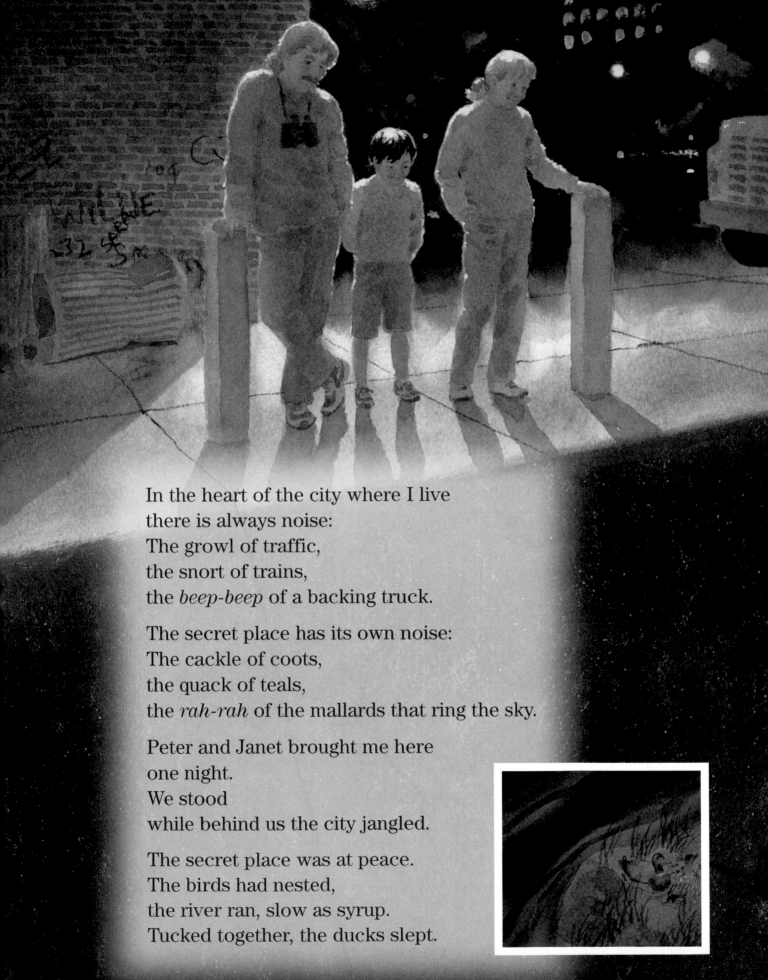

In the heart of the city where I live
there is always noise:
The growl of traffic,
the snort of trains,
the *beep-beep* of a backing truck.

The secret place has its own noise:
The cackle of coots,
the quack of teals,
the *rah-rah* of the mallards that ring the sky.

Peter and Janet brought me here
one night.
We stood
while behind us the city jangled.

The secret place was at peace.
The birds had nested,
the river ran, slow as syrup.
Tucked together, the ducks slept.

A coyote came
to lap the shadowed water.
A possum
carried her children to drink.

189

"How did they find this place?" I asked.
"They have always been here," Janet said.
"Before the city grew
there was wilderness.
This is all that's left.
Wild things need quiet.
We do, too."

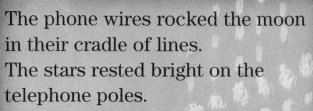

The phone wires rocked the moon
in their cradle of lines.
The stars rested bright on the
telephone poles.

"I want to tell everyone
what's here," I said.
"Be careful," Peter said.
"Some people might want
to take the secret place
and change it."

"I'd never want that to happen," I said.
"I told my father,
but he is good with secrets.
I will be careful who else I tell."

191

I will only say that
close to a freeway
and a railroad track
and tall smoking chimneys,
in the heart of the city where I live
there is a secret place.

192

If you can find it,
there may be ducklings.

Concept Connections

Linking the Selection

Think about the following questions, and then record your responses in the Response Journal section of your Writer's Notebook.

- Why did the boy in the story think he found a special place?

- Why is this secret place useful?

- Why did the boy decide to keep the secret place a secret?

Exploring Concept Vocabulary

The concept word for this lesson is **habitat.** If you do not know what this word means, look it up in a dictionary. Answer these questions:

- How is the river in the story like the wildlife's natural *habitat?*

- Think about where you live. How has wildlife adapted to your *habitat?*

Make up an oral sentence using the word *habitat* and one of the selection vocabulary words.

Expanding the Concept

Recall what you have learned from the selections in this unit. What conclusions can you draw about city wildlife?

Try to use the word *habitat* in your discussion. Add new ideas about city wildlife to the Concept/Question Board.

Meet the Author

Eve Bunting grew up in Ireland. Nine years after she got married, she and her family moved to the United States. She believes that the world is full of ideas for her stories. She writes about many of the events going on around her, as well as world events. *"I couldn't possibly write about all the interesting things I see. There aren't enough hours in the day,"* she says. Eve has used her ideas to write about horses running free, kings, sharks, whales, wildlife, and many other things.

Meet the Illustrator

Ted Rand began drawing holiday decorations in grade school. Once he graduated from high school, Rand drew advertisements for a department store and a newspaper. Rand also taught illustrating at the University of Washington. Now he devotes his time to illustrating children's books. *"I can honestly say that I have never enjoyed anything as much. There are so many challenges in the children's book field, that I have time for nothing else,"* he says.

Sometimes we are told to stop imagining things. Can we stop imagining things? Should we stop imagining things? How does your imagination work?

Through Grandpa's Eyes

Patricia MacLachlan
illustrated by Deborah Kogan Ray

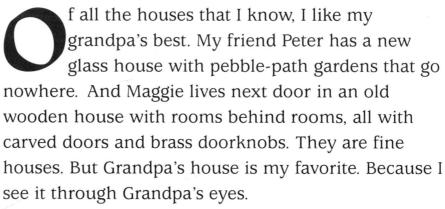

Of all the houses that I know, I like my grandpa's best. My friend Peter has a new glass house with pebble-path gardens that go nowhere. And Maggie lives next door in an old wooden house with rooms behind rooms, all with carved doors and brass doorknobs. They are fine houses. But Grandpa's house is my favorite. Because I see it through Grandpa's eyes.

Grandpa is blind. He doesn't see the house the way I do. He has his own way of seeing.

In the morning, the sun pushes through the curtains into my eyes. I burrow down into the covers to get away, but the light follows me. I give up, throw back the covers, and run to Grandpa's room.

The sun wakes Grandpa differently from the way it wakes me. He says it touches him, *warming* him awake. When I peek around the door, Grandpa is already up and doing his morning exercises. Bending and stretching by the bed. He stops and smiles because he hears me.

"Good morning, John."

"Where's Nana?" I ask him.

"Don't you know?" he says, bending and stretching. "Close your eyes, John, and look through my eyes."

I close my eyes. Down below, I hear the banging of pots and the sound of water running that I didn't hear before.

"Nana is in the kitchen, making breakfast," I say.

When I open my eyes again, I can see Grandpa nodding at me. He is tall with dark gray hair. And his eyes are sharp blue even though they are not sharp seeing.

I exercise with Grandpa. Up and down. Then I try to exercise with my eyes closed.

"One, two," says Grandpa, "three, four."

"Wait!" I cry. I am still on one, two when Grandpa is on three, four.

I fall sideways. Three times. Grandpa laughs as he hears my thumps on the carpet.

"Breakfast!" calls Nana from downstairs.

"I smell eggs frying," says Grandpa. He bends his head close to mine. "And buttered toast."

The wooden banister on the stairway has been worn smooth from Grandpa running his fingers up and down. I walk behind him, my fingers following Grandpa's smooth path.

We go into the kitchen.

"I smell flowers," says Grandpa.

"What flowers?" I ask.

He smiles. He loves guessing games.

"Not violets, John, not peonies . . ."

"Carnations!" I cry. *I* love guessing games.

"Silly." Grandpa laughs. "Marigolds. Right, Nana?"
Nana laughs, too.

"That's too easy," she says, putting two plates of food in front of us.

"It's not too easy," I protest. "How can Grandpa tell? All the smells mix together in the air."

"Close your eyes, John," says Nana. "Tell me what breakfast is."

"I smell the eggs. I smell the toast," I say, my eyes closed. "And something else. The something else doesn't smell good."

"*That* something else," says Nana, smiling, "is the marigolds."

When he eats, Grandpa's plate of food is a clock.

"Two eggs at nine o'clock and toast at two o'clock," says Nana to Grandpa. "And a dollop of jam."

"A dollop of jam," I tell Grandpa, "at six o'clock."

I make my plate of food a clock, too, and eat through Grandpa's eyes.

After breakfast, I follow Grandpa's path through the dining room to the living room, to the window that he opens to feel the weather outside, to the table where he finds his pipe, and to his cello in the corner.

"Will you play with me, John?" he asks.

He tunes our cellos without looking. I play with a music stand and music before me. I know all about sharps and flats. I see them on the music. But Grandpa plays them. They are in his fingers. For a moment I close my eyes and play through Grandpa's eyes. My fingering hand slides up and down the cello neck—toward the pegs for flats, toward the bridge for sharps. But with my eyes closed my bow falls from the strings.

"Listen," says Grandpa. "I'll play a piece I learned when I was your age. It was my favorite."

He plays the tune while I listen. That is the way Grandpa learns new pieces. By listening.

"Now," says Grandpa. "Let's do it together."

"That's fine," says Grandpa as we play. "But C sharp, John," he calls to me. "C sharp!"

Later, Nana brings out her clay to sculpt my
Grandpa's head.

"Sit still," she grumbles.

"I won't," he says, imitating her grumbly voice,
making us laugh.

While she works, Grandpa takes out his piece of
wood. He holds it when he's thinking. His fingers
move back and forth across the wood, making
smooth paths like the ones on the stair banister.

"Can I have a piece of thinking wood, too?" I ask.

Grandpa reaches in his shirt pocket and tosses a
small bit of wood in my direction. I catch it. It is
smooth with no splinters.

"The river is up," says Nana.

Grandpa nods a short nod. "It rained again last night. Did you hear the gurgling in the rain gutter?"

As they talk, my fingers begin a river on my thinking wood. The wood will winter in my pocket so when I am not at Grandpa's house I can still think about Nana, Grandpa, and the river.

When Nana is finished working, Grandpa runs his hand over the sculpture, his fingers soft and quick like butterflies.

"It looks like me," he says, surprised.

My eyes have already told me that it looks like Grandpa. But he shows me how to feel his face with my three middle fingers, and then the clay face.

"Pretend your fingers are water," he tells me.

My waterfall fingers flow down his clay head, filling in the spaces beneath the eyes like little pools before they flow down over the cheeks. It does feel like Grandpa. This time my fingers tell me.

Grandpa and I walk outside, through the front yard and across the field to the river. Grandpa has not been blind forever. He remembers in his mind the gleam of the sun on the river, the Queen Anne's lace in the meadow, and every dahlia in his garden. But he gently takes my elbow as we walk so that I can help show him the path.

"I feel a south wind," says Grandpa.

I can tell which way the wind is blowing because I see the way the tops of the trees lean. Grandpa tells by the feel of the meadow grasses and by the way his hair blows against his face.

When we come to the riverbank, I see that Nana was right. The water is high and has cut in by the willow tree. It flows around and among the roots of the tree, making paths. Paths like Grandpa's on the stair banister and on the thinking wood. I see a blackbird with a red patch on its wing sitting on a cattail. Without thinking, I point my finger.

"What is that bird, Grandpa?" I asked excitedly.

"*Conk-a-ree,*" the bird calls to us.

"A red-winged blackbird," says Grandpa promptly.

He can't see my finger pointing. But he hears the song of the bird.

"And somewhere behind the blackbird," he says listening, "a song sparrow."

I hear a scratchy song, and I look and look until I see the earth-colored bird that Grandpa knows is here.

Nana calls from the front porch of the house.

"Nana's made hot bread for lunch," he tells me happily. "And spice tea." Spice tea is his favorite.

I close my eyes, but all I can smell is the wet earth by the river.

As we walk back to the house, Grandpa stops suddenly. He bends his head to one side, listening. He points his finger upward.

"Honkers," he whispers.

I look up and see a flock of geese, high in the clouds, flying in a V.

"Canada geese," I tell him.

"Honkers," he insists. And we both laugh.

We walk up the path again and to the yard where Nana is painting the porch chairs. Grandpa smells the paint.

"What color, Nana?" he asks. "I cannot smell the color."

"Blue," I tell him, smiling. "Blue like the sky."

"Blue like the color of Grandpa's eyes," Nana says.

When he was younger, before I can remember, before he was blind, Grandpa did things the way I do. Now, when we drink tea and eat lunch on the porch, Grandpa pours his own cup of tea by putting his finger just inside the rim of the cup to tell him when it is full. He never burns his finger. Afterward, when I wash the dishes, he feels them as he dries them. He even sends some back for me to wash again.

"Next time," says Grandpa, pretending to be cross, "I wash, you dry."

In the afternoon, Grandpa, Nana, and I take our books outside to read under the apple tree. Grandpa reads his book with his fingers, feeling the raised Braille dots that tell him the words.

As he reads, Grandpa laughs out loud.

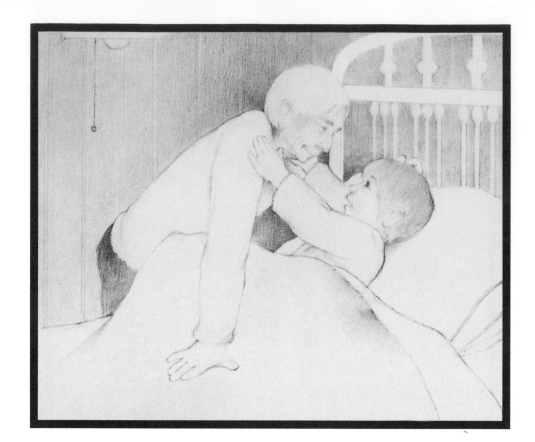

"Tell us what's funny," says Nana. "Read to us, Papa."

And he does.

Nana and I put down our books to listen. A gray squirrel comes down the trunk of the apple tree, tail high, and seems to listen, too. But Grandpa doesn't see him.

After supper, Grandpa turns on the television. I watch, but Grandpa listens, and the music and the words tell him when something is dangerous or funny, happy or sad.

Somehow, Grandpa knows when it is dark, and he takes me upstairs and tucks me into bed. He bends down to kiss me, his hands feeling my head.

"You need a haircut, John," he says.

Before Grandpa leaves, he pulls the light chain above my bed to turn out the light. But, by mistake, he's turned it on instead. I lie for a moment after he's gone, smiling, before I get up to turn off the light.

Then, when it is dark for me the way it is dark for Grandpa, I hear the night noises that Grandpa hears. The house creaking, the birds singing their last songs of the day, the wind rustling the tree outside my window.

Then, all of a sudden, I hear the sounds of geese overhead. They fly low over the house.

"Grandpa," I call softly, hoping he's heard them too.

"Honkers," he calls back.

"Go to sleep, John," says Nana.

Grandpa says her voice smiles to him. I test it.

"What?" I call to her.

"I said go to sleep," she answers.

She says it sternly. But Grandpa is right. Her voice smiles to me. I know. Because I'm looking through Grandpa's eyes.

Through Grandpa's Eyes

Concept Connections

Linking the Selection

Think about the following questions, and then record your responses in the Response Journal section of your Writer's Notebook.

- How did John's grandpa use his imagination?
- How did John use his imagination to see things through his grandpa's eyes?

Exploring Concept Vocabulary

The concept word for this lesson is *imagine.* If you do not know what this word means, look it up in a dictionary. Answer these questions:

- Why was it difficult for John to *imagine* things when he used only his eyes?
- How did John use his senses to *imagine* what Grandpa was seeing?

Use the word *imagine* and one of the selection vocabulary words to write a sentence in the vocabulary section of your Writer's Notebook.

Expanding the Concept

Think about the story "Through Grandpa's Eyes." What did you learn about imagination from this story?

Try to use the word *imagine* in your discussion.

Add new ideas about imagination to the Concept/Question Board.

Meet the Author

Patricia MacLachlan grew up in a family where reading was encouraged. She and her parents would read and discuss books and then act them out. When she was thirty-five, she began writing children's stories. Her most famous story is *Sarah, Plain and Tall*, but nearly all of her books have received awards and praise. Her concern for families makes its way into many of her books. She says, *"I see that I write books about brothers and sisters, about what makes up a family, what works and what is nurturing."*

Meet the Illustrator

Deborah Kogan Ray loved to play games with the other children in the alley behind the city street where she grew up. *"I was good at games, but,"* she says, *"I felt like an outsider. Mostly I loved to read and draw pictures."* When she was twelve she decided to be an artist. She took extra art classes and went on to college to study art. Deborah began illustrating and writing children's books while raising her two daughters.

The Apple

Arnold Adoff • *illustrated by Deborah Drummond*

The Apple
　　　　is on the top
branch
　　　of the tree
　　　　　touching
the
sky
　　　or the apple is
　　　　　　in
　　　the
　　　sky
touching
　　　　the top branch
　　　　　of the tree
and i am
　　　me on the ground
　　　waiting
　　　　　for
　　　　　　a
　　　good
　　　wind

214

Focus Questions What is it like to look at a familiar object and imagine it as something else? What other images do you see when looking at a house?

Houses

Aileen Fisher
illustrated by Deborah Drummond

Houses are faces
(haven't you found?)
with their hats in the air,
and their necks in the ground.

Windows are noses,
windows are eyes,
and doors are the mouths
of a suitable size.

And a porch—or the place
where porches begin—
is just like a mustache
shading the chin.

Focus Questions What do you think fog sees as it rolls across the land? Are the images that fog sees real or imagined? Explain.

Fog

Carl Sandburg
illustrated by Deborah Drummond

The Fog comes
on little cat feet.

It sits looking
over harbor and city
on silent haunches
and then moves on.

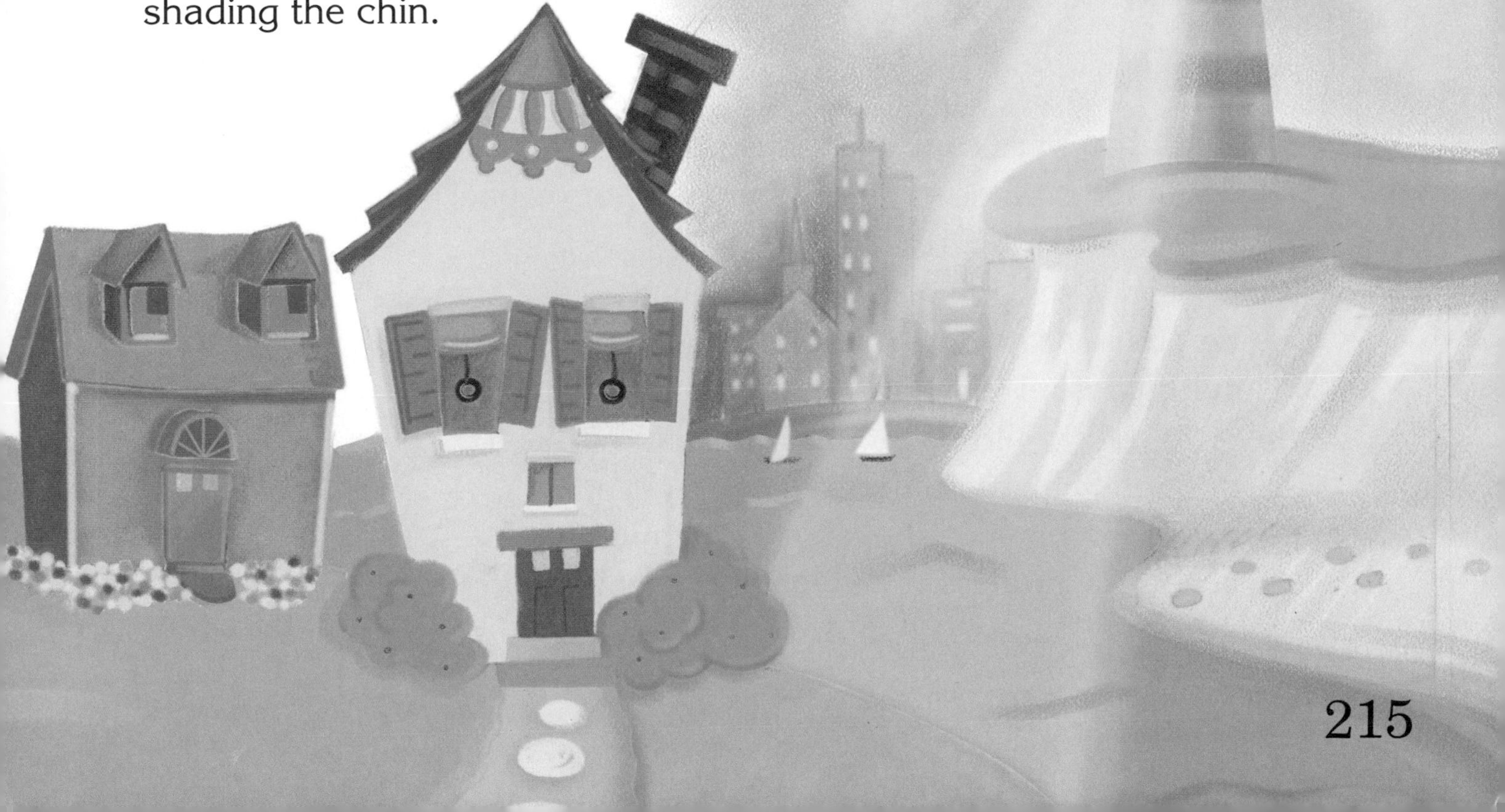

Focus Questions How can using your imagination help you see things in a new way? How can your life be more exciting and rewarding when you use your imagination?

The Cat Who Became a Poet

from *Nonstop Nonsense*
by Margaret Mahy
illustrated by Quentin Blake

A cat once caught a mouse, as cats do.

"Don't eat me," cried the mouse. "I am a poet with a poem to write."

"That doesn't make any difference to me," replied the cat. "It is a rule that cats must eat mice, and that is all there is to it."

"If only you'd listen to my poem you'd feel differently about it all," said the mouse.

"Okay," yawned the cat, "I don't mind hearing a poem, but I warn you, it won't make any difference."

So the mouse danced and sang:

> "The great mouse Night with the starry tail
> Slides over the hills and trees,
> Eating the crumbs in the corners of Day
> And nibbling the moon like cheese."

"Very good! That's very good!" the cat said. "But a poem is only a poem and cats still eat mice."

And he ate the mouse, as cats do.

Then he washed his paws and his face and curled up in a bed of catnip, tucking in his nose and his tail and his paws. Then he had a little cat nap.

Some time later he woke up in alarm.

"What's wrong with me?" he thought. "I feel so strange." He felt as if his head was full of colored lights. Pictures came and went behind his eyes. Things that were different seemed alike. Things that were real changed and became dreams.

"Horrakapotchkin!" thought the cat. "I want to write a poem."

He opened his mouth to meow, but a poem came out instead:

"The great Sun-Cat comes up in the east.
Lo! The glory of his whiskers touches the hills.
Behold! the fire of his smiling
Burns on the oceans of the rolling world."

"Cat-curses!" said the cat to himself. "I have turned into a poet, but I don't want to make poetry. I just want to be a cat catching mice and sleeping in the catnip bed. I will have to ask the witch about this."

The cat went to the witch's crooked house. The witch sat at the window with her head in her hands. Her dreams turned into black butterflies and flew out of the window.

She took the cat's temperature and gave him some magic medicine that tasted of dandelions.

"Now talk!" she commanded.

The cat opened his mouth to ask her if he was cured. Instead he found himself saying:

"Lying in the catnip bed,
The flowering cherry over my head,
Am I really the cat that I seem?
Or only a cat in another cat's dream?"

"I'm afraid it is too late," said the witch. "Your case is hopeless. Poetry has got into your blood and you're stuck with it for the rest of your life."

"Horrakapotchkin!" cried the cat sadly, and he started off home.

But, five houses away from his own house, a black dog called Max chased him, as dogs do, and the cat had to run up a tree. He boxed with his paw at Max and went to hiss and spit at him, but instead he found himself saying:

"Colonel Dog fires his cannon
And puts his white soldiers on parade.
He guards the house from cats, burglars
And any threat of peacefulness."

The dog Max stopped and stared. "What did you call me? Colonel Dog? I like that. But what do you mean, I fire my cannon?"

"That's your barking," said the cat.

"And what do you mean, I put my white soldiers on parade?" asked the dog again.

"That's your teeth," said the cat.

The dog wagged his tail. "I like the way you put it," he said again. "How did you learn to talk like that?"

"Oh, it's poetry," said the cat carelessly. "I am a poet, you see."

"Well, I'll tell you what! I'll let you go without barking at you if I may come and hear that poem again sometimes," the dog Max said, still wagging his tail. "Perhaps I could bring some other dogs to hear it too. Colonel Dog, eh? White soldiers, eh? Very true." And he let the cat go on home to his catnip bed.

"If only he knew," the cat thought. "I wasn't meaning to praise him. Poetry is very tricky stuff and can be taken two ways."

The cat went on thinking. "I became a poet through eating the mouse. Perhaps the mouse became a poet through eating seeds. Perhaps all this poetry stuff is just the world's way of talking about itself." And straight away he felt another poem coming into his mind.

"Just time for a sleep first," he muttered into his whiskers. "One thing, I'll never eat another poet again. One is quite enough." And he curled up in the catnip bed for a quick kip-and-catnap, as cats do.

The Cat Who Became a Poet

Concept Connections

Linking the Selection

 Think about the following questions, and then record your responses in the Response Journal section of your Writer's Notebook.

- The cat really began to use his imagination after he became a poet. How could you tell he was using his imagination?

- Why did the cat say poetry is tricky stuff?

Exploring Concept Vocabulary

The concept word for this lesson is *enrich*. If you do not know what this word means, look it up in a dictionary. Answer these questions:

- What kinds of things can *enrich* the imagination? What kinds of things *enrich* your imagination?

- How did eating the mouse *enrich* the cat's imagination?

Make up an oral sentence using the word *enrich* and one of the selection vocabulary words.

Expanding the Concept

Think about John in the story "Through Grandpa's Eyes" and the cat in "The Cat Who Became a Poet." How were the ways John and the cat used their imaginations similar? How were they different?

Try to use the word *enrich* in your discussion of the characters. Add new ideas about imagination to the Concept/Question Board.

Meet the Author

Margaret Mahy was born and raised in New Zealand. She has worked as a librarian and writes children's books. She says that she knew she wanted to write *"from the time I was seven onwards . . . I decided in childhood that I wanted to be a writer, and I used to write in little notebooks, which I also illustrated."* She has written well over 100 books for young readers, as well as several for young adult readers.

Meet the Illustrator

Quentin Blake was born and raised in England. He is an author, illustrator, teacher, and editor. Quentin Blake has illustrated more than 200 books. He has also been awarded the Hans Christian Andersen Award for Illustration. Quentin Blake has some words of advice for young artists: *"You must want to draw all the time, because that is the only way you can get good at it. You can study a certain amount of technique, but doing it is the key element."*

A CLOAK for the DREAMER

Aileen Friedman
illustrated by Kim Howard

Once there was a tailor who had three fine sons. The tailor loved his sons and appreciated their helpfulness.

Ivan, the oldest son, picked up all the pins from the floor of his father's shop and gathered together all the little pieces of loose thread. Whenever he could, Ivan watched his father measure, cut, and sew. He wanted to be a tailor himself one day and work alongside his father.

Alex, the middle son, brought his father bolts of fabric to cut and then carefully put them away. Whenever he could, Alex practiced sewing together the small, leftover pieces of fabric. He, too, wanted to be a tailor and work alongside his father.

Misha, the youngest son, carried the finished jackets and cloaks and dresses to his father's customers all over town. Whenever he could, he stopped at the bookseller's shop around the corner. There, he pored over maps of the world and pictures of faraway places. Unlike his brothers, Misha did not want to be a tailor and work alongside his father. He dreamed instead of traveling far and wide, and of making his own way in the world.

One morning, the tailor gathered his three sons before him. "Now is the time," he said, "for each of you to show that you can do the work of a tailor.

"Our good customer, the Archduke, leaves on an important journey in just three days. For this journey, he has ordered three new cloaks for himself and three dresses for his wife. I can sew the dresses, but, to get the job done on time, each of you must make one cloak."

The sons were glad to help their father and listened carefully to his instructions.

"First of all," explained the tailor, "the Archduke wants his cloaks to be very colorful. Every bolt of fabric we have is of just one color, so each of you will have to cut pieces from many bolts and sew them into a single colorful cloth of your own design. Of course, the cloak you fashion from your cloth will also have to protect the Archduke from the wind and the rain. Work by yourselves, so that all three cloaks will be different."

The sons got busy right away.

Ivan first studied the bolts of fabric. He had
seen his father use them all at one time or
another, so he cut a rectangle from each one.
Then, using the pattern of bricks on the floor,
Ivan carefully sewed the rectangles together.
From this beautiful cloth of many colors, he
fashioned a cloak for the Archduke. Ivan was
ready on the morning of the third day to present
the cloak to his father.

Meanwhile, Alex had thought of the colors of the Archduke's carriage and the coat of arms that was painted on its side. He pulled down the bolts of red, yellow, and purple fabric and cut many squares from each bolt. He nimbly stitched the squares together to make one beautiful cloth of the Archduke's colors, then fashioned the cloth into a sturdy cloak. Because of all his sewing practice, Alex worked quickly enough to have his cloak ready by the morning of the second day.

With a day to spare, Alex had time to worry. "Perhaps my cloak isn't interesting enough," he thought. "Perhaps the Archduke would want something more." He thought again of the Archduke's coat of arms and the pattern of its background. Then he went back to work.

Alex cut more red, yellow, and purple squares, but this time he snipped them in half on the diagonal. He sewed these triangles together to match the pattern on the Archduke's coat of arms, and fashioned this new cloth into another cloak. Alex sewed even faster than he had the first time, and the second cloak was ready on the morning of the third day.

All the while, Misha was working, too. He thought of going out into the world as he cut circles from the bolts of fabric. He picked his colors from the maps he loved—blue for the deep oceans and winding rivers, green for the meadows of the countryside, yellow for the sands of the deserts, red for the routes between faraway places.

Misha sewed his circles together, carefully joining them where they met, and the cloth he made was beautiful. But when he held it up to the light, Misha saw that it was full of open spaces. He could tell this cloth wouldn't make a proper cloak, but he did not have time to start over. Although he worried that the cloak would disappoint his father, Misha completed it in time.

On the morning of the third day, when the tailor had sewn the last stitch on the third dress for the Archduke's wife, he called for his sons to bring in their cloaks.

Ivan proudly showed his cloak of many-colored rectangles.

"You have made a beautiful cloak, Ivan," said the tailor. "I am honored to present it to the Archduke. From now on, you will be a tailor, too, and work alongside your father."

Happy for his brother, but still unsure of his own work, Alex showed his two cloaks to his father.

"Why, Alex," said the tailor, "you have made *two* beautiful cloaks! How thoughtful of you to use the Archduke's own colors. He will be thrilled to wear these, I'm sure. And your quick, even stitches show me that you, too, are ready to be a tailor and work alongside your father."

"Now, Misha," he said, turning to his youngest son, "let me see the cloak you have made."

"I'm afraid I did not do it right, Father," said Misha. He showed his cloak of circles and open spaces.

The tailor looked at his son's cloak and, for a long time, said nothing. He was thinking of what his friend, the bookseller, had told him. Finally, he spoke.

"The cloak is beautiful, Misha," said the tailor. "The colors remind me of deep oceans and winding rivers, green meadows and golden deserts, and the long routes between faraway places.

"But, it's true that this cloak will not keep out the wind and the rain. We cannot sell it to the Archduke. Still," he added, "no harm is done. Ivan and Alex have made the three cloaks we need."

Then the tailor smiled at his youngest son. "Perhaps you were not meant to be a tailor," he said. "But, you know that already, don't you?"

"Yes, Father," answered Misha.

"I see your dreams of traveling the world in all the circles of your cloak," continued the tailor. "Do you think it is time for you to cross these oceans and rivers, meadows and deserts, and to follow these routes to faraway places?"

"Yes, Father," answered Misha.

"Then take these cloaks and dresses to the Archduke, and come back to get ready for your own journey. Tomorrow your brothers and I will send you off into the world."

That night the tailor sat in his little shop, looking sadly at his third son's beautiful, but useless, cloak. Though he knew Misha had to leave home, he hated to see him go. He knew Ivan and Alex felt just as bad as he did.

"If only we could give Misha something to protect him as he makes his own way in the world," the tailor thought. He sat by the fire a little longer, and then he had an idea.

The tailor ran up the stairs and quietly woke Ivan and Alex.

"I know what we can give Misha to take on his journey into the world," whispered the tailor. "We can make him a new cloak from his own cloak of circles. That way, it will have all the colors of his dreams, but it will be sewn together in the practical way tailors sew things—and it will protect him from the wind and the rain."

"But how, Father?" asked Ivan. "The circles won't fit together."

"I know, my son," said the tailor. He motioned for his sons to follow him downstairs to the shop. There he explained how it could be done.

All night long the tailor and his two oldest sons worked on Misha's cloak. Ivan snipped the circles apart, and his father trimmed them into hexagons. As his father cut, Alex quickly sewed the hexagons together to make one cloth of the dreamer's colors. When the cloth was finished, the three tailors fashioned it into a strong and beautiful cloak. They stitched the last stitch as the sun came up on the day Misha was to leave home.

Later that morning, the tailor and his sons Ivan and Alex kissed and hugged Misha good-bye at the door of their little shop. Then they stood together and watched as the dreamer set off into the world, his beautiful cloak growing smaller and smaller in the distance.

A CLOAK for the DREAMER

Concept Connections

Linking the Selection

Think about the following questions, and then record your responses in the Response Journal section of your Writer's Notebook.

- How did Misha use his imagination to make a cloak for the Archduke? Why was the cloak useless?

- How did Misha's father use his imagination to turn the useless cloak of circles into a useful cloak?

Exploring Concept Vocabulary

The concept word for this lesson is *creative.* If you do not know what this word means, look it up in a dictionary. Answer these questions:

- How is the word *creative* related to imagination?

- How did each boy's cloak show that he was *creative?*

Write the following sentence beginning. Then choose a selection vocabulary word, and write your own ending to complete the sentence.

One of the boys made a *creative* cloak by _____ .

Expanding the Concept

Compare Misha in "A Cloak for the Dreamer" to Grandpa in "Through Grandpa's Eyes." How were the ways these characters used their imaginations alike and different?

Try to use the word *creative* in your discussion.

Add new ideas about imagination to the Concept/Question Board.

236

Meet the Author

Aileen Friedman is much like the character of Misha in the selection, "A Cloak for the Dreamer," because she, too, plans to travel to distant places. She enjoys writing stories about independence. Friedman's advice for students is to make quiet time to listen to the stories everyone has in their heads. She says, *"Think about why things happen, why people do things, why things are the way they are. These imaginings will give you ideas for stories."* Friedman was born in Maryland and currently lives in California. After graduating from college in New York with honors, she became a third-grade teacher for a year before starting her career in publishing.

Meet the Illustrator

Kim Howard grew up the daughter of a mathematician. After working as a waitress, model, actress, and textile-designer, she committed herself to being a full-time illustrator. She moved from Sacramento, California, to Ketchum, Idaho. Howard attended the University of California at Berkeley, where she earned a degree in drama and painting.

Cow Triptych. 1974. **Roy Lichtenstein.** Oil on canvas, 3 panels, each 68" × 62". ©Roy Lichtenstein/Licensed by VAGA, New York, NY.

Time Transfixed. 1938. **René Magritte.** Oil on Canvas. 146.1 × 97.5 cm. The Art Institute of Chicago. ©2001 C. Herscovici, Brussels/Artist Right Society (ARS), New York.

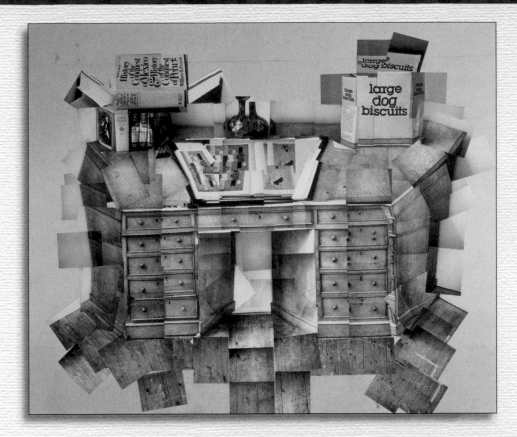

The Desk. July 1st,
1984. **David Hockney.**
Photographic collage.
$48 \frac{1}{2}$ " $\times 46 \frac{1}{2}$".
Collection of the artist.
©David Hockney.

Baird Trogon. 1985. **Robert Lostutter.** Watercolor over
graphite. 61.5 × 88 cm. The Art Institute of Chicago.

Focus Questions How can you turn something from your imagination into something that others can see, hear, touch, or taste? Have you ever created an object from your imagination? If so, explain. If not, what would you like to create?

Picasso

from the book by Mike Venezia

Pablo Picasso was one of the greatest artists of the twentieth century. He was born in Malaga, Spain, in 1881, and died in France in 1973.

Picasso's father was an art teacher at the local school. He encouraged his son to paint and draw. He wanted Picasso to become a great artist some day.

Picasso's painting style changed over the period of his life more than any other great artist. He was always trying new and different things.

The painting at the right was done when he was only fifteen years old.

Portrait of the Artist's Mother (Maria Picasso Lopez). 1896. Pablo Picasso.

Oil on canvas. Museo Picasso, Barcelona. ©2001 Estate of Pablo Picasso / Artists Rights Society (ARS), New York.

Portrait of Dora Maar. 1937. Pablo Picasso.

Oil on canvas. Musée Picasso, Paris. ©2001 Estate of Pablo Picasso / Artists Rights Society (ARS), New York.

This painting was done when Picasso was fifty-six.

There's quite a difference between the two paintings, isn't there?

When Picasso was nineteen, he left Spain and went to Paris, France. Some of the first paintings he did there look a little bit like the work of other famous French artists.

This painting below reminds many people of the work done by Toulouse-Lautrec. Some of Picasso's other early paintings remind people of van Gogh, Gauguin, and Monet.

Le Moulin de la Galette. Autumn 1900. Pablo Picasso.

Oil on canvas. Solomon R. Guggenheim Museum. ©2001 Estate of Pablo Picasso / Artists Rights Society (ARS), New York.

The Blue Period

Then something happened! Picasso's paintings changed. His work became different from anyone else's.

His best friend died, and Picasso felt alone and sad. At the same time, none of his paintings were selling, and he was almost starving to death.

Because of his mood, Picasso began to paint with lots of blue (blue can be a very sad color). He made all the people in his paintings look lonely and sad.

Some people thought Picasso's blue paintings were great. Others (including Picasso's father) thought they were just too strange. This meant his paintings were controversial.

The Old Guitarist. 1903. Pablo Picasso.

Oil on panel. 122.9 × 82.6 cm. The Art Institute of Chicago. ©2001 Estate of Pablo Picasso / Artists Rights Society (ARS), New York.

The Rose Period

Picasso's Blue Period ended when he met a girl named Fernande. Fernande and Picasso fell in love, and soon a happier color started showing up in Picasso's paintings. This was the beginning of the Rose Period.

Not only were Picasso's colors happier during the Rose Period, but he started painting happier things. Picasso painted a lot of circus people during this time. He often painted them with their animals.

The Rose Period didn't last very long, though, because Picasso found a new way to paint that was really exciting and different.

Family of Saltimbanques. 1905. Pablo Picasso.

Portrait of D.H. Kahnweiler. 1910. Pablo Picasso.

Oil on canvas. 100.6 × 72.8 cm. The Art Institute of Chicago. ©2001 Estate of Pablo Picasso / Artists Rights Society (ARS), New York.

Weeping Woman. 1937. Pablo Picasso.

Oil on canvas. Tate Gallery, London. ©2001 Estate of Pablo Picasso / Artists Rights Society (ARS), New York.

Cubism

Cubism was the next style of painting that Picasso developed and made famous. The painting on the left is a cubist painting of one of Picasso's friends. The man in the painting looks like he's been broken up into little cubes. That's where the name cubism came from.

Look closely. Can you see the man's face, what he was wearing, his hands, a bottle, a glass, and maybe his pet cat? Can you find anything else?

Cubism is one of the most important periods in the history of modern art.

For hundreds of years, artists tried very hard to paint things so they would look real. Then Picasso came along and started to paint people and things that didn't look the way people and things were supposed to look.

Picasso was always shocking people, but when he started painting people who had eyes and noses in the wrong places—well, even some of his closest friends thought he had gone too far.

Picasso kept working with cubism and changed it over the years. It became much more colorful and flatter looking. It also became easier to see what Picasso was painting.

In the painting below, *Three Musicians*, you can see the three musicians, and tell what instruments they're playing.

Three Musicians. Fontainebleau, Summer 1921. Pablo Picasso.

Oil on canvas, 6'7" × 7'3 $\frac{3}{4}$". The Museum of Modern Art, New York. ©2001 Estate of Pablo Picasso / Artists Rights Society (ARS), New York.

In another style that popped up for a while, Picasso painted people who looked more real again. Picasso had just visited Rome, a city filled with statues and monuments. When he returned from his trip, he did a series of paintings in which people look like they've been chiseled out of stone, like statues.

Many of Picasso's paintings look funny because of the way he moves eyes, noses, and chins around. The amazing thing about these paintings is how much they look like the real person.

Portrait of Jaime Sabartés as Hidalgo. 1939.
Pablo Picasso.

Oil on canvas. Museo Picasso, Barcelona. ©2001 Estate of Pablo Picasso /
Artists Rights Society (ARS), New York.

Jaime Sabartés, painted by Steve
Dobson, from a photograph by
Gilberte Brassai.

Look at the painting of Picasso's best friend, Jaime
Sabartés. Does it look like the same man shown in the
smaller painting to the right?

The thing that made Picasso such a great artist was
his originality. He had the imagination to try new and
different things through his entire life.

Picasso lived to be ninety-two years old. He was a great painter, but he was great at other things, too.

He made sculptures, prints, drawings, beautifully colored dishes and bowls. He even made costumes and scenery for plays.

It's a lot of fun to see real Picasso paintings. You'll be surprised at how big some of them are. Look for his paintings in your art museum.

Most of the pictures in this biography came from the museums listed below. If none of these museums is close to you, maybe you can visit one when you are on vacation.

- The Museum of Modern Art, New York, New York
- Solomon R. Guggenheim Museum, New York, New York
- The Art Institute, Chicago, Illinois
- National Gallery of Art, Washington, D. C.
- Picasso Museum, Barcelona, Spain
- Musée Picasso, Paris, France

Ape and Her Child. 1952. Pablo Picasso.
Bronze. Musée Picasso, Paris. ©2001 Estate of Pablo Picasso / Artists Rights Society (ARS), New York.

Portrait of Aunt Pepa. c.1895–96. Pablo Picasso.
Oil on canvas. Museo Picasso, Barcelona. ©2001 Estate of Pablo Picasso / Artists Rights Society (ARS), New York.

Picasso

Concept Connections

Linking the Selection

Think about the following questions, and then record your responses in the Response Journal section of your Writer's Notebook.

- Picasso's art changed a lot over the years. What does this tell you about his imagination?

- How did Picasso use cubism to show his imagination?

Exploring Concept Vocabulary

The concept word for this lesson is *inspiration.* If you do not know what this word means, look it up in a dictionary. Answer these questions:

- How does *inspiration* affect the imagination?

- What feelings were Picasso's *inspiration* during the Blue Period? What feelings were his *inspiration* during the Rose Period?

In the Vocabulary section of your Writer's Notebook, write a sentence using the word *inspiration* and one of the selection vocabulary words.

Expanding the Concept

How were Misha in "A Cloak for the Dreamer" and Picasso alike in showing their imaginations? How were they different?

Try to use the word *inspiration* in your discussion of the characters.

Add new ideas about imagination to the Concept/Question Board.

Meet the Author

Mike Venezia studied art at the
school of the Art Institute in Chicago. He
thinks the best way for children to learn
about art and artists is through fun. *"If
children can look at art in a fun way
and think of artists as real people, the
exciting world of art will be open to them
for the rest of their lives."*

Focus Questions Have you ever wanted something so much that you actually believed it existed, even if it didn't? Explain. How can you use your imagination to help you achieve a goal?

The Emperor's New Clothes

by Hans Christian Andersen
retold and illustrated by
Nadine Bernard Westcott

There once lived an emperor who was very fond of new clothes. While other kings might like to parade their soldiers or spend an evening at the theater, there was nothing this emperor loved more than trying on new clothes—which his servants would bring him in great stacks, morning, noon, and night.

Other servants toiled endlessly to keep the emperor's vast wardrobe cleaned and pressed. The kingdom's most learned scholars were kept constantly on hand to advise him on his choice of clothing. Any outfit the emperor might desire must be ready for him at a moment's notice.

The emperor had a different outfit for every hour of the day, and clothes for each day of the week.

For no matter how great or small the occasion, he wanted to wear just the right clothes to make his subjects see him as a wise and able ruler.

But his outfits never seemed quite right.

And his clothes were apt to turn up in the most inconvenient places.

Not even his wife or his most trusted ministers could persuade him that he need not worry so much about his royal attire.

One day, two swindlers traveled to the castle, pretending to be weavers.

"We can weave the most beautiful cloth imaginable!" the first told the emperor. "And, what is more, the clothes made from our fabrics are invisible to anyone who is either foolish or unfit for his office."

"Not everyone, of course, is able to wear such finery," added the second. "But they are obviously the perfect clothes for a wise ruler like yourself!"

The emperor thought of how wisely he could rule his people if only he had such an outfit. "Why, not only would I look grand, but with those clothes on, I could find out which of my ministers is unfit for his post; I could tell the wise from the foolish. This cloth must be woven for me at once!"

The weavers set up their looms and worked late into the night.

No one was allowed to see their work, until…the emperor sent his wisest and most trusted minister to see what had been made.

The weavers begged the minister to step closer. They named all the colors, and described the pattern in great detail. The minister paid close attention to all they said, for, unable to believe his own eyes, he wanted to be able to repeat it exactly to the emperor.

The minister hurried back and described the new clothes to the emperor, exactly as they had been described to him.

"Why, you must wear them tomorrow in the royal procession!" the emperor's wife cried. "It is the perfect chance to show all of your subjects what a wise and magnificent ruler you are."

The next morning the weavers at last announced, "The clothes are finished!" They brought in the royal robes and dressed the emperor in them, taking great care to see that there were no loose threads and that the royal garments hung just right. The emperor could scarcely believe his eyes, but he kept quiet as a mouse, lest his subjects think him a fool.

People had come from every corner of the kingdom to see the magnificent new clothes.

As the emperor set forth in the royal procession, the crowd grew silent. *My new clothes must be so stunning, no one can find the right words to praise them!* thought the emperor. He lifted his head and marched on proudly, until…a small child's voice could be heard clearly to say, "But he has no clothes on!"

"He has no clothes on!" the people echoed, each feeling secretly foolish not to have spoken up earlier.

What could the emperor possibly do now?

Without any of his royal outfits to help him look intelligent or brave, the emperor realized it was more important now than ever to act like a king. He lifted his head even higher, and stood even taller, and continued the procession. Never had he felt so foolish … but never had he acted so wisely.

Seeing their ruler's extraordinary courage, the crowd began to cheer, more loudly than the emperor had ever heard them.

"Long live the king!"

The Emperor's New Clothes

Concept Connections

Linking the Selection

Think about the following questions, and then record your responses in the Response Journal section of your Writer's Notebook.

- Why did the swindlers want the emperor and his trusted ministers to use their imaginations?

- How did the people of the kingdom use their imaginations during the parade?

Exploring Concept Vocabulary

The concept word for this lesson is **illusion.** If you do not know what this word means, look it up in a dictionary. Answer these questions:

- How can a person's imagination allow him or her to create an **illusion?**

- How did the swindlers use their imaginations to create the **illusion** of fine clothing?

Make up an oral sentence that includes the word **illusion** and one of the selection vocabulary words.

Expanding the Concept

Think about the selections you have read in this unit. How was the way the characters in "The Emperor's New Clothes" used their imaginations different from the ways other characters used their imaginations?

Try to use the word **illusion** in your discussion.

Add new ideas about imagination to the Concept/Question Board.

Meet the Author

Hans Christian Andersen was born into a
poor family in Odense, Denmark, in 1805. His
father, a shoemaker, often read to his son and
took him to see plays. When they did not have
enough money to see a play, Andersen would read
the playbill and imagine what the play and
characters were like. In his lifetime, he wrote more
than 150 fairy tales, in addition to poems, plays,
novels, and travel books. Andersen wrote on many
subjects, sometimes writing about what he was feeling. When he was a
schoolboy, he was sad because other children made fun of his long nose.
He later wrote "The Ugly Duckling" based on those feelings. Hans
Christian Andersen was known for writing with wisdom and humor
about the goodness of common
people and common objects.

Meet the Author and Illustrator

Nadine Bernard Westcott won second
prize in a coloring contest featured on the back of a
cereal box when she was young. Throughout her
childhood, she doodled on the back of paper
placemats and napkins. A large portion of Westcott's
career has been as an illustrator in the greeting card
industry. During this time, she began adapting and
illustrating children's books. The primary goal of her
children's books is to have the children identify with
the characters and to laugh.

Focus Questions Have you ever imagined that the playground, your backyard, or your bedroom is a different place? What places do you imagine they are? What do you do in your imaginary worlds?

Roxaboxen

Alice McLerran
illustrated by Barbara Cooney

Marian called it Roxaboxen. (She always knew the name of everything.) There across the road, it looked like any rocky hill—nothing but sand and rocks, some old wooden boxes, cactus and greasewood and thorny ocotillo—but it was a special place.

The street between Roxaboxen and the houses curved like a river, so Marian named it the River Rhode. After that you had to ford a river to reach Roxaboxen.

Of course all of Marian's sisters came: Anna May and Frances and little Jean. Charles from next door, even though he was twelve. Oh, and

Eleanor, naturally, and Jamie with his brother
Paul. Later on there were others, but these were
the first.

Well, not really the first. Roxaboxen had
always been there and must have belonged to
others, long before.

When Marian dug up a tin box filled with
round black pebbles everyone knew what it
was: it was a buried treasure. Those pebbles
were the money of Roxaboxen. You could still

find others like them if you looked hard enough. So some days became treasure-hunting days, with everybody trying to find that special kind. And then on other days you might just find one without even looking.

A town of Roxaboxen began to grow, traced in lines of stone: Main Street first, edged with the whitest ones, and then the houses. Charles made his of the biggest stones. After all, he was the oldest. At first the houses were very plain, but soon they all began to add more rooms. The old wooden boxes could be shelves or tables or anything you wanted. You could find pieces of pottery for dishes. Round pieces were best.

Later on there was a town hall. Marian was mayor, of course; that was just the way she was. Nobody minded.

After a while they added other streets. Frances moved to one of them and built herself a new house outlined in desert glass, bits of amber, amethyst, and sea-green: A house of jewels.

And because everybody had plenty of money, there were plenty of shops. Jean helped Anna May in the bakery—pies and cakes and bread baked warm in the sun. There were two ice cream parlors. Was Paul's ice cream the best, or Eleanor's? Everybody kept trying them both. (In Roxaboxen you can eat all the ice cream you want.)

Everybody had a car. All you needed was
something round for a steering wheel. Of course,
if you broke the speed limit you had to go to jail.
The jail had cactus on the floor to make it
uncomfortable, and Jamie was the policeman.
Anna May, quiet little Anna May, was always
speeding—you'd think she liked to go to jail.

But ah, if you had a horse, you could go as fast
as the wind. There were no speed limits for
horses, and you didn't have to stay on the
roads.

All you needed for a horse was a stick and
some kind of bridle, and you could gallop
anywhere.

264

Sometimes there were wars. Once there was a great war, boys against girls. Charles and Marian were the generals. The girls had Fort Irene, and they were all girl scouts. The boys made a fort at the other end of Roxaboxen, and they were all bandits.

Oh, the raids were fierce, loud with whooping and the stamping of horses! The whirling swords of ocotillo had sharp thorns—but when you reached your fort you were safe.

Roxaboxen had a cemetery, in case anyone died, but the only grave in it was for a dead lizard. Each year when the cactus bloomed, they decorated the grave with flowers.

Sometimes in the winter, when everybody was
at school and the weather was bad, no one went
to Roxaboxen at all, not for weeks and weeks.
But it didn't matter; Roxaboxen was always
waiting. Roxaboxen was always there. And
spring came, and the ocotillo blossomed, and
everybody sucked the honey from its flowers,
and everybody built new rooms, and everybody
decided to have jeweled windows. That summer
there were three new houses on the east slope
and two new shops on Main Street.

And so it went. The seasons changed, and the
years went by. Roxaboxen was always there.

266

The years went by, and the seasons changed, until at last the friends had all grown tall, and one by one, they moved away to other houses, to other towns. So you might think that was the end of Roxaboxen—but oh, no.

Because none of them ever forgot Roxaboxen. Not one of them ever forgot. Years later, Marian's children listened to stories of that place and fell asleep dreaming dreams of Roxaboxen. Gray-haired Charles picked up a black pebble on the beach and stood holding it, remembering Roxaboxen.

More than fifty years later, Frances went back and Roxaboxen was still there. She could see the white stones bordering Main Street, and there where she had built her house the desert glass still glowed—amethyst, amber, and sea-green.

Roxaboxen

Concept Connections

Linking the Selection

Think about the following questions, and then record your responses in the Response Journal section of your Writer's Notebook.

- What is Roxaboxen?

- How did the children use their imaginations in Roxaboxen?

Exploring Concept Vocabulary

The concept word for this lesson is *imaginary.* If you do not know what this word means, look it up in a dictionary. Answer these questions:

- What *imaginary* things did the children create in Roxaboxen?

- What *imaginary* things have you created using your imagination?

Make up an oral sentence using the word *imaginary* and one of the selection vocabulary words.

Expanding the Concept

Recall what you have learned about imagination from the selections in this unit. What ideas about imagination were the same throughout the selections? What ideas were different? What conclusions can you draw about imagination?

Try to use the word *imaginary* in your discussion.

Add new ideas about imagination to the Concept/Question Board.

Meet the Author

Alice McLerran has had many jobs and gone to some of the best colleges in the country. She was raised in an army family and says that *"home throughout my childhood shifted every year or so—from Hawaii to Germany, from New York to Ecuador."* In addition to writing, she has worked in the Andes Mountains as an anthropologist and has also been a teacher.

Meet the Illustrator

Barbara Cooney was born in the hotel her grandfather built in New York. Her great-grandfather and mother were also artists, but the only art lesson she received from her mother was how to clean paintbrushes.

She often used people and images from her own life when she illustrated books. She won Caldecott Awards for *Chanticleer and the Fox* and for *Ox-Cart Man*. Barbara Cooney created art to bring enjoyment to herself and others, and to make the world a more beautiful place.

Focus Questions What is the sun like on a sunny day?
What is the sun like on a cloudy day? How can
the sun change your mood?

The sun is a yellow-tipped porcupine. . .

Crow Indian Poem
illustrated by Tricia Courtney

The sun is a yellow-tipped porcupine

Lolloping through the sky,

Nibbling treetops and grasses and weeds,

Floating on rivers and ponds,

Casting shining barbed quills at the earth.

Pronunciation Key

a as in **a**t

ā as in l**a**te

â as in c**a**re

ä as in f**a**ther

e as in s**e**t

ē as in m**e**

i as in **i**t

ī as in k**i**te

o as in **o**x

ō as in r**o**se

ô as in b**ou**ght and r**a**w

oi as in c**oi**n

o͝o as in b**oo**k

o͞o as in t**oo**

or as in f**or**m

ou as in **ou**t

u as in **u**p

ū as in **u**se

ûr as in t**ur**n; g**er**m, l**ear**n, f**ir**m, w**or**k

ə as in **a**bout, chick**e**n, penc**i**l, cann**o**n, circ**u**s

ch as in **ch**air

hw as in w**h**ich

ng as in ri**ng**

sh as in **sh**op

th as in **th**in

t͟h as in **th**ere

zh as in trea**s**ure

The mark (´) is placed after a syllable with a heavy accent, as in **chicken** (**chik**´ ən).

The mark (ˊ) after a syllable shows a lighter accent, as in **disappear** (**dis**´ ə pēr´).

Glossary

A

abandon (ə ban´ dən) *v.* To leave empty.

absorb (ab sorb´) *v.* To soak up.

abundantly (ə bun´ dənt lē) *adv.* With more than enough; richly; well.

abuse (ə būs´) *n.* Unkind or cruel words or actions.

adapt (ə dapt´) *v.* To fit in.

adequate (ad´ i kwit) *adj.* As much as needed; enough.

adorn (ə dorn´) *v.* To decorate.

ailanthus tree (ā lan´ thəs trē´) *n.* A wide-spreading tree with long leaves and thick clusters of flowers.

alarm (ə lärm´) *n.* Sudden fear; a sense of danger.

alert (ə lûrt´) *v.* To warn or make aware of.

amber (am´ bər) *n.* A yellowish-brown color.

amethyst (am´ ə thist) *n.* A purple color.

anxiously (angk´ shəs lē) *adv.* With a worried or uneasy feeling.

ao dai (ow zī) *n. Vietnamese.* A garment worn by females in Vietnam, usually for special occasions.

apathetic (ap´ ə thet´ ik) *adj.* Not interested; not caring about something.

aphid (ā´ fid) *n.* A tiny insect that lives on the juice of plants.

appoint (ə point´) *v.* To name officially.

appreciate (ə prē´ shē āt´) *v.* To understand the nature of.

arctic (ärk´ tik) *adj.* Having to do with the area around the North Pole.

arrange (ə rānj´) *v.* To take steps to make something happen.

astonish (ə stä´ nish) *v.* To surprise or amaze.

auburn (ô´ bərn) *adj.* Reddish-brown.

audible (ô´ də bəl) *adj.* Loud enough to be heard.

B

bandit (ban´ dit) *n.* A robber; a thief.

Pronunciation Key: at; lāte; câre; fäther; set; mē; it; kīte; ox; rōse; ô in bought; coin; bŏŏk; tōō; form; out; up; ūse; tûrn; ə sound in about, chicken, pencil, cannon, circus; chair; hw in which; ring; shop; thin; *th*ere; zh in treasure.

banister (ban´ ə stər) *n.* The railing on a staircase.

barbed (bärbd) *adj.* With a sharp point.

bargain (bär´ gən) *n.* A deal or agreement between two people or parties.

beautiful (bū´ ti fəl) *adj.* Lovely; pleasing to look at.

beckon (bek´ ən) *v.* To invite someone by waving.

binoculars (bə no´ kyə lərz) *n.* A device to help see objects that are far away.

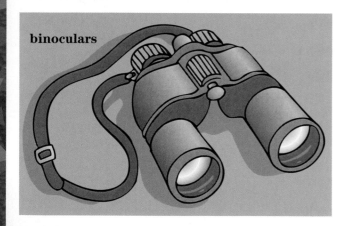

binoculars

biologist (bī ol´ ə jist) *n.* A person who studies plants and animals.

blossom (blä´ səm) *v.* To bloom; to produce flowers.

blunt (blunt) *adj.* Having a dull or thick edge.

bolster (bōl´ stər) *v.* To support; to make stronger.

border (bor´ dər) *v.* To touch at the edge or boundary.

bow (bō´) *n.* A wooden rod with horsehair stretched from end to end used in playing a stringed instrument.

Braille (brāl) *n.* A system of printing with raised dots that stand for letters. Blind people read Braille by touching the dots.

bridle (brīd´ l) *n.* The part of a horse's harness that goes over its head.

bridle

buck (bək) *n.* A male deer.

burdock (bûr´ dok) *n.* A weed with coarse, broad leaves and prickly heads or burs.

burglar (bər´ glər) *n.* A person who steals; a thief.

burrow (bər´ō´) *v.* To make a snug, warm place, usually deep and narrow, like a tunnel that a rabbit or gopher digs.

burst (bərst´) *v.* To be filled and overflowing with strong emotion.

C

camouflage (kam´ ə fläzh´) *v.* To disguise; to hide.

cartwheel (kärt´ hwēl´) *n.* A jump made by landing on the hands and then the feet, turning like a wheel.

carve (kärv´) *v.* To cut carefully.

cast (kast) *v.* To throw.

catnip (kat´ nip) *n.* A spicy-smelling plant that cats like.

cavity (kav´ i tē) *n.* A small hole; a hollow.

champion (cham´ pē ən) *n.* 1. A person who stands up for a cause or for others. 2. One who wins first place.

chant (chant) *v.* To sing or repeat words as a group.

chao buoi sang (chow bwē sung) *Vietnamese.* Good morning.

chisel (chiz´ əl) *v.* To cut with a metal tool.

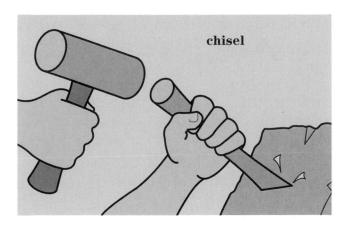

chisel

chive (chīv) *n.* A small plant related to leeks and onions.

chore (chor) *n.* A small job.

circulate (sûr´ kyə lāt´) *v.* To pass around.

clamor (klam´ ər) *n.* A loud, lengthy noise.

cloak (klōk) *n.* A loose-fitting coat that is worn over the shoulders.

clutch (kluch) *n.* A group of eggs to be hatched.

collection (kə lek´ shən) *n.* An assortment of similar things gathered together to study or to show to others.

colonel (kûr´ nl) *n.* An officer in the army, marines, or air force.

command (kə mand´) *v.* To order. —*n.* A short, firm instruction.

commute (kə myo͞ot´) *v.* To travel between two places every day.

compete (kəm pēt´) *v.* To try to win by striving against another person or people.

complex (kom´ pleks) *n.* A group of related things.

concrete (kän´ krēt´) *n.* A strong building material that hardens as it dries. —*adj.* Made of concrete.

content (kən tent´) *adj.* Satisfied; pleased.

controversial (kon´ trə vûr´ shəl) *adj.* Causing arguments or different opinions.

275

> **Pronunciation Key:** at; lāte; câre; fäther; set; mē; it; kīte; ox; rōse; ô in bought; coin; bŏŏk; tōō; form; out; up; ūse; tûrn; ə sound in about, chicken, pencil, cannon, circus; chair; hw in which; ring; shop; thin; there; zh in treasure.

corkscrew (kork′ skrōō′) *v.* To move by turning back and forth or twisting.

courtyard (kort′ yärd′) *n.* An open area with walls around it that is next to a large building.

cozy (kō′ zē) *adj.* Warm and comfortable.

cranny (kran′ ē) *n.* A slit; a narrow opening.

creed (krēd) *n.* The statement of a person's belief or faith.

crevice (krev′ is) *n.* A crack.

crinkle (kring′ kəl) *v.* To wrinkle.

crop (kräp) *n.* A plant grown for food or to sell to make money.

cubism (kū′ biz əm) *n.* A style of painting in which the picture is formed by cubes or square shapes.

curious (kyur′ ē əs) *adj.* Interested in knowing.

D

dahlia (dal′ yə) *n.* A plant with showy, bright-colored flowers.

dangle (dang′ gəl) *v.* To hang down loosely.

dart (därt) *v.* To move or run quickly from one place to another.

debris (də brē′) *n.* Rubbish; trash.

decorate (de′ kə rāt′) *v.* To add ornamentation; to adorn or make beautiful.

delighted (di lī′ təd) *adj.* Very happy; pleased.

depression (di presh′ ən) *n.* 1. A shallow hole or a dent. 2. A period of time when business is slow and people are out of work.

desert (di zərt′) *v.* To leave or abandon.

design (di zīn′) *n.* A plan for putting something together.

desire (di zīr′) *v.* To have a strong wish for.

despite (di spīt′) *prep.* In spite of; regardless of.

diagonal (dī a′ gə nəl) *n.* A line connecting two opposite angles on a four-sided shape.

discard (di skärd′) *v.* To throw away.

disgrace (dis grās′) *v.* To act badly; to shame.

dither (dith′ ər) *n.* An upset, confused feeling.

doe (dō) *n.* A female deer.

dollop (dol′ əp) *n.* A blob of something; a small amount of something.

dweller (dwel′ ər) *n.* Someone who lives in a certain place.

dwelling (dwel´ ing) *n.* A place to live.

E

emperor (em´ pər ər) *n.* A man who rules an empire.

encourage (en kûr´ ij) *v.* To urge or inspire someone to do something.

enormous (i nor´ məs) *adj.* Very large; huge or massive.

environment (en vī´ rən mənt) *n.* Everything surrounding a plant, animal, or person.

exercise (ek´ sər sīz´) *n.* A physical activity for the sake of fitness.

exhaust (ig zôst´) *n.* The gases and smoke from a car that go into the air.

exist (ig zist´) *v.* To be or to continue to be.

experiment (ik sper´ ə mənt) *n.* A test used to discover something.

exploration (ek´ splə rā´ shən) *n.* The act of searching or looking closely at a new area.

extraordinary (ik stror´ dn er´ ē) *adj.* Rare; not ordinary.

F

fabric (fa´ brik) *n.* Material used to make clothing.

falcon (fôl´ kən) *n.* A powerful bird of prey.

fashion (fa´ shən) *v.* To create.

faze (fāz) *v.* To bother.

finery (fīn´ rē) *n.* Fancy or dressy clothing.

flat (flat) *n.* A musical note that sounds one-half tone lower than it usually does.

flatter (flat´ ər) *adj.* More flat. —*v.* To compliment.

flimsy (flim´ zē) *adj.* Weak; slight; breakable.

flourish (flûr´ ish) *v.* To grow well; to succeed.

ford (ford) *v.* To cross a river or stream.

forklift (for´ klift´) *n.* A small truck with a lifting device on the front so that things can be easily picked up and moved.

forklift

fragrant (frā´ grənt) *adj.* Sweet-smelling.

freight (frāt) *n.* Products and materials that are transported by trains, boats, or planes.

277

Pronunciation Key: at; lāte; câre; fäther; set; mē; it; kīte; ox; rōse; ô in bought; coin; boŏk; toō; form; out; up; ūse; tûrn; ə sound in about, chicken, pencil, cannon, circus; chair; hw in which; ring; shop; thin; there; zh in treasure.

G

gamble (gam′ bəl) *n.* A risk; a chance.

garment (gär′ mənt) *n.* An item of clothing.

gleam (glēm) *v.* To be bright and shiny.

Gothic (goth′ ik) *adj.* A style of art that uses much detail and decoration.

graduation (gra′ jə wā′ shən) *n.* A ceremony to mark the completion of a full course of study.

graze (grāz) *v.* To eat or feed on grasses.

greasewood (grēs′ woŏd′) *n.* A woody plant that grows in the dry West.

grim (grim) *adj.* Stern; harsh.

gutter (gut′ ər) *n.* A curved path or trough for carrying off rainwater.

H

habitat (hab′ i tat′) *n.* The natural surroundings of a plant or animal.

haunch (hônch) *n.* The hip and the thickest part of the thigh.

hedge (hej) *n.* A row of bushes used as a fence.

height (hīt) *n.* The distance from the top to the bottom of something.

hexagon (hek′ sə gän′) *n.* A six-sided shape with six angles.

hinge (hinj) *n.* A metal joint that attaches a door to its frame and lets the door move.

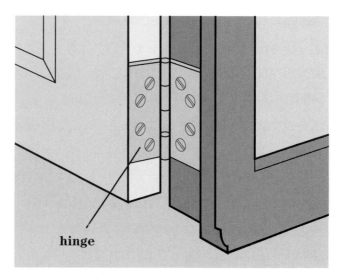

hinge

hoa-phuong (hwä fung) *n.* *Vietnamese.* A tropical flower in Vietnam that has groups of red blossoms.

honorable (ä′ nər ə bəl) *adj.* Deserving of honor or respect.

hoof (hoŏf) *n.* A hard covering on the feet of animals such as horses and cows.

hostility (ho stil′ i tē) *n.* Unfriendliness; willingness to fight.

hover (huv′ ər) *v.* To hang in the air near something.

humiliation (hū mil′ ē ā′ shən) *n.* An action or event that hurts someone's pride.

I

imagination (i maj′ ə nā′ shən) *n.* The ability to create new ideas in one's mind.

imitate (im′ i tāt′) *v.* To copy.

immature (im′ ə cho͞or′) *adj.* Not fully grown.

inconvenient (in′ kən vē′ nyənt) *adj.* Causing difficulty.

initially (i nish′ əl lē) *adv.* At first.

intersection (in′ tər sek′ shən) *n.* The place where two streets cross each other.

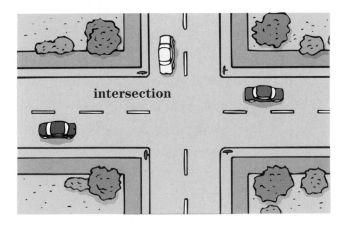

intersection

intruder (in tro͞o′ dər) *n.* Someone who enters a place against the owner's will.

island (ī′ lənd) *n.* 1. A piece of land surrounded by water. 2. Anything surrounded by something else.

intimidate (in tim′ i dāt′) *v.* To threaten; to try to scare.

J

jangle (jang′ gəl) *v.* To make a harsh sound, like two pieces of metal hitting each other.

jiggle (jig′ əl) *v.* To move back and forth quickly.

jostle (jos′ əl) *v.* To bump into.

journey (jər′ nē) *n.* A trip.

K

kip (kip) *n.* A nap; sleep.

L

laboratory (la′ bə rə tōr′ ē) *n.* A place where science studies and experiments are done.

launch (lônch) *v.* To begin.

lollop (lä′ ləp) *v.* To move in a slow, lazy way.

lonely (lōn′ lē) *adj.* Sad from being alone.

loom (lo͞om) *n.* A machine that weaves thread into cloth.

loyalty (loi′ əl tē′) *n.* The quality of being faithful to a person or cause.

M

magnificent (mag ni′ fə sənt) *adj.* Of grand character and beauty; wonderful.

Pronunciation Key: at; lāte; câre; fäther; set; me; it; kīte; ox; rōse; ô in bought; coin; bŏŏk; tōō; form; out; up; ūse; tûrn; ə sound in about, chicken, pencil, cannon, circus; chair; hw in which; ring; shop; thin; there; zh in treasure.

manners (ma´ nərz) *n.* Habits of behavior.

margin (mär´ jin) *n.* The blank edge of a paper.

marvelous (märv´ ə ləs) *adj.* Outstanding.

mayor (mā´ ər) *n.* The chief elected official of a city.

metallic (mə tal´ ik) *adj.* As if made of metal.

microscope (mī´ krə skōp´) *n.* An instrument that makes small things look larger.

microscope

migrate (mī´ grāt) *v.* To move from colder to warmer lands and back again.

miniature (min´ ē ə chər) *adj.* Tiny; very small.

molt (mōlt) *v.* To lose or shed hair, feathers, or a shell.

monument (mon´ yə mənt) *n.* Anything built to honor a person or event.

monument

mood (mōōd) *n.* A general state of mind.

mottled (mot´ ld) *adj.* Spotted or blotched with different colors.

mound (mound) *n.* A pile or heap of something.

mustache (mus´ tash) *n.* Hair grown on the upper lip.

N

nervous (nər´ vəs) *adj.* Moving in an excited or jumpy way.

nest (nest) *v.* To build a home. —*n.* A shelter made by animals; a home.

nestling (nest´ ling) *n.* A bird too young to leave the nest.

nibble (ni´ bəl) *v.* To take small bites.

nimbly (nim′ blē) *adv.* Quickly and easily.

nook (nŏŏk) *n.* A small, hidden place.

O

observation (ob′ zûr vā′ shən) *n.* The act of studying or noticing.

observe (əb zûrv′) *v.* To see; to look at.

occasion (ə kā′ zhən) *n.* An event.

ocotillo (ō′ kə tēl′ yō) *n.* A desert bush with sharp spines.

opportunity (op′ ər tŏŏ′ ni tē) *n.* A good chance.

ordinary (ôr′ dən er′ ē) *adj.* The usual kind.

organization (or′ gə nə zā′ shən) *n.* A group of people who join together for one purpose; a club.

originality (ə rij′ ə nal′ i tē) *n.* Newness; freshness.

originally (ə rij′ ə nl ē) *adv.* At first; in the beginning.

outfit (out′ fit′) *n.* A group of people with a common purpose or belief.

overpass (ō′ vər pas′) *n.* A road that crosses above another road.

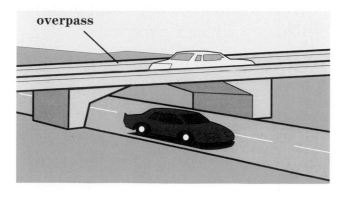
overpass

P

parachute (par′ ə shŏŏt′) *n.* An umbrella-shaped object that helps other objects float down slowly from heights.

parade (pə rād′) *v.* To march in an orderly fashion.

parasite (par′ ə sīt′) *n.* An animal that lives and feeds on another animal.

patch (pach) *n.* A small area.

particular (pər tik′ yə lər) *adj.* Only; special.

patient (pā′ shənt) *adj.* Calmly putting up with something difficult.

passageway (pas′ ij wā′) *n.* A narrow place to walk between two buildings.

pattern (pat′ ərn) *n.* The way in which things are placed.

peer (pēr) *v.* To look.

peregrine (per′i grin) *n.* A type of falcon that catches other birds in flight.

period (pēr′ ē əd) *n.* An amount of time.

permission (pər mi′ shən) *n.* Consent that allows one to do something.

petition (pə tish′ ən) *n.* A written request to someone in charge, signed by those who agree.

Pronunciation Key: at; lāte; câre; fäther; set; mē; it; kīte; ox; rōse; ô in bought; coin; boŏk; toō; form; out; up; ūse; tûrn; ə sound in about, chicken, pencil, cannon, circus; chair; hw in which; ring; shop; thin; there; zh in treasure.

petroleum jelly (pe´ trō´ lē əm jel´ ē) *n.* A greasy, sticky substance used to coat things.

plantain (plan´ tin) *n.* A weed that has large leaves and long spikes with small flowers.

plaster (plas´ tər) *n.* A substance like cement that is used to make walls and ceilings.

plume (ploōm) *n.* A long feather.

poet (pō´ ət) *n.* A person who writes or composes poems.

pollution (pə loō´ shən) *n.* Harmful or dirty material added to the air, water, or soil.

population (pä´ pyə lā´ shən) *n.* A count of how many in a group.

porcupine (por´ kyə pīne) *n.* An animal with stiff pointy hairs.

portion (por´ shən) *n.* A part.

possess (pə zes´) *v.* To have; to own.

post (pōst) *n.* A position that one is appointed to.

pottery (pot´ ə rē) *n.* Bowls, pots, plates, and other objects shaped from moist clay and hardened by heat.

practical (prak´ ti kəl) *adj.* Useful.

prejudice (prej´ ə dis) *n.* Unfairness; an opinion formed without knowing the facts.

prickly (prik´ lē) *adj.* Full of sharp points that stick or sting.

privet (priv´ it) *n.* A shrub related to the lilac bush and the olive tree. It has small white flowers and smooth, dark fruit; all parts are poisonous.

probably (prä´ bə blē) *adv.* Most likely to happen.

procession (prə se´ shən) *n.* A group of people that moves along in a formal manner.

proclaim (prō klām) *v.* To declare; to announce officially.

proper (pro´ pər) *adj.* Acceptable.

protest (prō´ test´) *n.* A statement against something.

proud (proud) *adj.* Feeling very pleased with something.

provoke (prə vōk´) *v.* To cause.

Q

Queen Anne's lace (kwēn´ anz´ lās´) *n.* A wild form of the carrot plant with lacy white flowers.

quill (kwil) *n.* The stiff pointy hairs on a porcupine.

R

racial (rā´ shəl) *adj.* Having to do with a race of people.

rebel (ri bəl´) *v.* To resist a ruler's power.

rectangle (rek´ tan´ gəl) *n.* A four-sided shape with four right angles.

regardless (ri gärd´ lis) *adv.* Without concern for.

relocate (rē lō´ kāt´) *v.* To move to a different place.

rescue (res´ kū´) *v.* To save from harm or danger.

resist (ri zist´) *v.* To fight against.

respond (ri spond´) *v.* To answer.

responsibility (ri spon´ sə bil´ i tē) *n.* A duty; a job.

rotate (rō´ tāt´) *v.* To move as though going around in a circle.

routine (rōō tēn´) *n.* The same actions done over and over.

royal (roi´ əl) *adj.* Owned by a king or a queen.

S

scenery (sē´ nə rē) *n.* The painted pictures and objects used on stage in a play.

scholar (sko´ lər) *n.* A person who has learned a great deal about a subject.

scrawl (skrôl) *v.* To write in a fast, messy way. —*n.* A scribble.

sculpt (skulpt) *v.* To make a figure, statue, or design by carving wood or stone or by forming clay.

sculpture (skulp´ chər) *n.* A figure, statue, or design carved out of something solid.

sculpture

segregation (seg´ ri gā´ shən) *n.* Keeping different races of people apart from each other.

seldom (sel´ dəm) *adv.* Rarely; not often.

sensitive (sen´ si tiv) *adj.* Able to feel things well.

seriously (sir´ ē əs lē) *adv.* Thoughtfully, sincerely.

sesame (ses´ə mē) *n.* The seed of an Asian plant which is used to add flavor to food.

severe (sə vir´) *adj.* Harsh or extreme.

sewer (sōō´ ər) *n.* An underground pipe that carries dirty water away from buildings.

shades (shādz) *n.* Sunglasses.

shadowed (sha´ dōd) *adj.* Covered in shadow; partially hidden.

shallow (shal´ ō) *adj.* Being close to the bottom; not deep.

sharp (shärp) *n.* A musical note that sounds one-half tone higher than it usually does. —*adj.* 1. Clear. 2. Keen.

shock (shok) *v.* To surprise and upset at the same time.

shutter (shut´ ər) *n.* A doorlike cover that opens and closes over a window.

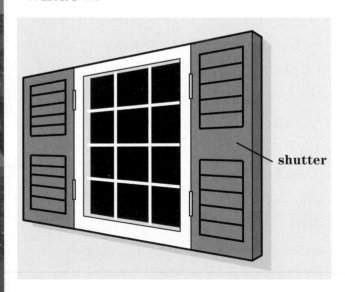

shutter

skyscraper (skī´ skrā´ pər) *n.* A very tall building found in a city.

slope (slōp) *n.* An upward or downward slant.

smokestack (smōk´ stak´) *n.* A large, tall chimney from which smoke is released.

smokestack

soar (sor) *v.* To fly at a great height.

solemnly (so´ ləm lē) *adv.* In a serious way.

solution (sə lōō´ shən) *n.* A way to solve a problem.

sought (sôt) *v.* Past tense of **seek:** To look for.

species (spē´ shēz) *n.* An animal family; a kind of animal.

splinter (splin´ tər) *n.* A small sharp piece of wood broken off from a larger piece.

squeegee (skwē´ jē) *v.* To make a squeaking sound by rubbing as if using a squeegee, which is a rubber-edged tool for removing excess water from windows.

squiggle (skwig´ əl) *n.* A line that is curved or wavy.

stalk (stôk) *n.* The stem of a plant.

starve (stärv) *v.* To die from hunger.

statue (stach′ ōō) *n.* A carved figure of a person or an animal.

sternly (stûrn′ lē) *adv.* In a strict or harsh way.

stiff (stif) *adj.* Something not easily bent; not flexible.

stitch (stich) *v.* To join two pieces of cloth together with tight loops of thread.

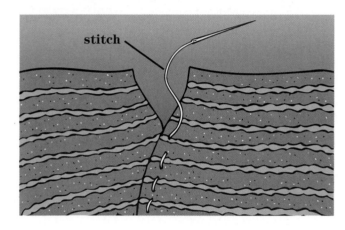
stitch

stout (stout) *adj.* Sturdy; strong.

stucco (stuk′ ō) *n.* Plaster that covers outside walls.

sturdy (stər′ dē) *adj.* Solidly built.

style (stīl) *n.* The way something is done.

subject (səb′ jikt) *n.* A person who is ruled over.

suburb (sub′ ûrb) *n.* A town on the outer edge of a larger city.

suitable (sōō′ tə bəl) *adj.* Fitting; right.

sycamore (sik′ ə mor′) *n.* A shade tree; a buttonwood tree.

T

taunt (tônt) *n.* Spoken words that make fun of someone in a mean way.

tease (tēz) *v.* To annoy continuously.

temperature (tem′ pər ə chər) *n.* The hotness or coldness of a thing.

territory (ter′ ə tor′ ē) *n.* An area of land.

toil (toi′ əl) *v.* To work hard.

trace (trās) *v.* To form carefully; to sketch.

trainer (trā′ nər) *n.* Teacher, coach.

traitor (trā′ tər) *n.* Someone who betrays another's trust.

triangle (trī′ an′ gəl) *n.* A three-sided shape with three angles.

trestle (tres′ əl) *n.* A framework that holds up train tracks above a river or above the ground.

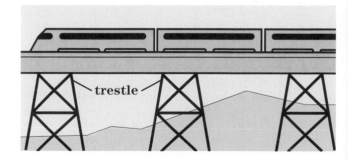
trestle

trill (tril) *v.* To make a vibrating sound, like the sound some birds make.

> **Pronunciation Key: a**t; l**ā**te; c**â**re; f**ä**ther;
> s**e**t; m**ē**; **i**t; k**ī**te; **o**x; r**ō**se; **ô** in b**ou**ght;
> c**oi**n; b**oo**k; t**oo**; f**o**rm; **ou**t; **u**p; **u**se; t**û**rn;
> **ə** sound in **a**bout, chick**e**n, penc**i**l,
> cann**o**n, circ**u**s; **ch**air; **hw** in **wh**ich; ri**ng**;
> **sh**op; **th**in; **th**ere; **zh** in trea**s**ure.

tundra (tun´ drə) *n.* In the arctic regions, a flat plain with no trees.

twitter (twi´ tər) *v.* To chatter noisily; to sound like chirping birds.

tyrant (tī´ rənt) *n.* A harsh, unjust ruler.

U

urban (ûr´ bən) *adj.* In a city.

V

vacant (vā´ kənt) *adj.* Empty.

vigilante (vij´ ə lan´ tē) *n.* A person who acts as if he or she is the law.

violently (vī´ ə lənt lē) *adv.* With destructive force.

visible (viz´ ə bəl) *adj.* Able to be seen.

W

wardrobe (wor´ drōb´) *n.* A collection of clothes.

warehouse (war´ hous´) *n.* A building where products and materials are stored.

whine (hwīn) *v.* To talk in a complaining, annoying voice.

wilderness (wil´ dər nəs) *n.* A wild, natural area that has not been developed or occupied by people.

windswept (wind´ swept´) *adj.* Blown by wind constantly.

Photo Credits